200
Casseroles

**Stephanie Ashcraft
and Janet Eyring**

GIBBS SMITH
TO ENRICH AND INSPIRE HUMANKIND

To my family. —S.A.

To my husband, Sean, thank you for your computer and eagle-eye proofreading skills. —J.E.

First Edition
15 14 13 12 11   5 4 3 2 1

Text © 2011 by Stephanie Ashcraft and Janet Eyring

Published by
Gibbs Smith
P.O. Box 667
Layton, Utah 84041

1.800.835.4993 orders
www.gibbs-smith.com

Designed by Renee Bond
Printed and bound in China
Gibbs Smith books are printed on either recycled, 100% post-consumer waste, FSC-certified papers or on paper produced from a 100% certified sustainable forest/controlled wood source.

Library of Congress Cataloging-in-Publication Data:

Ashcraft, Stephanie.
  200 casseroles / Stephanie Ashcraft and Janet Eyring. -- 1st ed.
      p. cm.
   ISBN 978-1-4236-2334-2
1. Casserole cooking. 2. Cookbooks. I. Eyring, Janet. II. Title. III.
Title: Two hundred casseroles.
   TX693.A85 2011
   641.8'21--dc23
                                    2011013852

Contents

Helpful
Hints

1. Always grease casserole pans or dishes with nonstick cooking spray for quick cleanup.

2. For the best results, use ceramic, glass, or stoneware baking dishes.

3. Bake casseroles on the middle oven rack. If possible, avoid the top and bottom racks.

4. The first time you try a recipe, check the casserole 5 minutes before its minimum cooking time. Each oven heats differently.

5. Many casseroles can be assembled the night before and stored in the refrigerator. Remove casserole from the refrigerator 20 minutes before baking.

6. Many casseroles can be assembled and frozen for use at a later date. Move the casserole from the freezer to the refrigerator 24 hours before baking. If casserole was frozen, it may take 10–15 minutes longer to bake. Bake until the temperature at the center of the casserole reaches 160 degrees.

7. Avoid freezing casseroles that contain pasta or rice.

8. Low-fat, light, or low-sodium ingredients can be substituted in any recipe.

9. When using aluminum foil to cover casseroles, place the shiny side down toward the food. If the shiny side is facing up, it may reflect the heat and possibly increase cooking time.

10. Always cook the casserole in a preheated oven.

11. Condensed cream of chicken, cream of mushroom, and cream of celery soups can be used interchangeably.

12. Precook chicken in large quantities and freeze in 1-cup increments to save preparation time.

Breakfast

Blueberry French Toast Casserole

Makes 6 servings.

1 (20-ounce) loaf bread, cubed
1 (8-ounce) package cream cheese, cubed
1 cup fresh or frozen blueberries
12 eggs, beaten
2 cups milk
1 teaspoon vanilla
1 1/3 cups maple syrup
Powdered sugar
Maple or blueberry syrup

Place half the bread cubes in a greased 9 x 13-inch pan. Layer cream cheese cubes evenly over bread. Sprinkle blueberries over top. Cover with the remaining bread cubes.

In a large bowl, whisk together the eggs, milk, vanilla, and syrup. Drizzle the egg mixture evenly over bread. Cover and refrigerate 2 hours or overnight; remove 30 minutes prior to baking.

Preheat oven to 350 degrees. Let casserole come to room temperature, then cover with aluminum foil and bake 30 minutes. Uncover and bake 25–30 minutes more, or until center is firm and top is golden brown. Lightly dust casserole with the powdered sugar. Serve with blueberry or maple syrup.

Raspberry French Toast Bake

Makes 6–8 *servings.*

1/2 cup flour
1 1/2 cups whole milk
2 tablespoons sugar
1 teaspoon vanilla
6 eggs
10 slices bread, cubed
4 ounces cream cheese,
   cubed
1 cup fresh or frozen
   raspberries (if
   using frozen, do
   not defrost!)
1 cup chopped pecans
2 tablespoons sugar
1/2 teaspoon cinnamon
Powdered sugar for
   garnish

In a large bowl, whisk together the flour, milk, 2 tablespoons sugar, vanilla, and eggs. Add the cubed bread to egg mixture. Pour into a greased 9 x 13-inch pan and sprinkle the cream cheese and raspberries over top. Cover tightly and refrigerate for up to 24 hours; remove 30 minutes prior to baking.

Preheat oven to 350 degrees. In a small bowl, combine the pecans, 2 tablespoons sugar, and cinnamon. Sprinkle over the casserole. Cover with aluminum foil and bake 30 minutes. Uncover and bake 25–30 minutes more, or until center is firm and top is golden brown. Dust with powdered sugar before serving.

Cinnamon Raisin French Toast Casserole

Makes 6 *servings.*

1 (24-ounce) loaf
   cinnamon raisin
   bread, cubed
6 eggs, slightly beaten
3 cups milk
2 teaspoons vanilla
Powdered sugar
Maple syrup

Place bread cubes into a greased 9 x 13-inch pan.

In a bowl, whisk together the eggs, milk, and vanilla. Pour egg mixture evenly over bread. Cover and refrigerate 2 hours or overnight. Remove from refrigerator 20 minutes before baking.

Preheat oven to 350 degrees. Bake uncovered for 45–50 minutes, or until golden brown. Sprinkle powdered sugar and drizzle with maple syrup.

Apple-Cranberry Casserole

Makes 6–8 *servings.*

1 (21-ounce) can apple
    pie filling
1 (14-ounce) can whole-
    berry cranberry
    sauce
$1/4$ cup butter, softened
$1^{1}/2$ cups rolled oats
$2/3$ cup brown sugar
1 teaspoon cinnamon
French toast or pancakes

Preheat oven to 350 degrees.

Combine the pie filling and cranberry sauce in a 1-quart bowl. Spread the apple-cranberry mixture into an 8 x 8-inch pan prepared with nonstick cooking spray.

In a separate bowl, use a fork to mix together the butter, oats, brown sugar, and cinnamon until crumbly. Sprinkle evenly over top. Bake for 35–40 minutes, or until golden brown and crisp. Serve over French toast or pancakes.

Asparagus English Muffin Bake

Makes 6–8 *servings.*

1 pound fresh asparagus, cut into 1-inch pieces
5 English muffins, split and toasted
2 cups grated Colby Jack cheese, divided
1½ cups diced fully cooked ham
1½ cups chopped red bell pepper
8 eggs, beaten
2 cups milk
1 teaspoon salt
1 teaspoon dry mustard
1½ teaspoons black pepper

In a 4-quart saucepan, boil the asparagus pieces for 1 minute; drain and put into a large bowl of ice water to stop the cooking process. Remove and pat asparagus dry with paper towels.

Place the English muffin halves cut side up to form a crust in the bottom of a greased 9 x 13-inch pan. Cut the muffins to fill the empty spaces in the pan as needed. Layer the asparagus, half the cheese, ham, and bell pepper over the muffins.

In a large bowl, whisk together the eggs, milk, salt, dry mustard, and pepper. Pour the egg mixture evenly over ham and cheese layer. Cover and refrigerate 2 hours or overnight. Remove from refrigerator 30 minutes before preheating the oven to 375 degrees. Bake for 40–45 minutes, or until set in the center. Immediately sprinkle remaining cheese over top and serve.

Baked Breakfast Burritos

Makes 6–8 *servings.*

12 eggs
³/₄ cup chunky salsa
10 medium flour tortillas
1 (4-ounce) can chopped
    green chiles
1 cup grated cheddar
    cheese

Preheat oven to 350 degrees.

In a frying pan, scramble the eggs and salsa together until firm but not dry. Heat the tortillas in the microwave until softened. Put a spoonful of scrambled egg mixture in the middle of each tortilla. Roll up tortillas and place in a greased 9 x 13-inch pan. Sprinkle with green chiles and cheese. Cover with aluminum foil and bake 15 minutes.

NOTE: Cook and crumble spicy sausage into the scrambled eggs for a heartier breakfast.

Scrambled Egg and Ham Pizza

Makes 6–8 *servings.*

1 (13.8-ounce) tube refrigerated pizza crust dough
8 eggs
2 tablespoons milk
Salt and pepper, to taste
1½ cups diced fully cooked ham
1 cup grated cheddar cheese

Preheat oven to 400 degrees.

Spread the pizza dough along the bottom and halfway up the sides of a greased 9 x 13-inch pan. Bake for 8 minutes.

In a frying pan, scramble and cook the eggs and milk until firm but not dry. Season with salt and pepper. Spread scrambled eggs over the hot crust. Place ham and cheese evenly over the eggs. Bake for 8–12 minutes, or until crust is golden brown and cheese is melted.

Ham and Cheese Breakfast Bake

Makes 6–8 *servings.*

12 eggs
1 cup milk
1/2 teaspoon pepper
**2 cups diced fully
     cooked ham**
**1/2 cup chopped green
     onion**
**2/3 cup chopped green
     bell pepper**
**1 1/2 cups grated medium
     or sharp cheese**

Preheat oven to 350 degrees.

In a 2-quart bowl, whisk together the eggs until smooth; mix in the milk and pepper. Stir in the ham, green onion, bell pepper, and half the cheese. Pour the egg mixture into a 9 x 13-inch pan prepared with nonstick cooking spray. Bake for 45 minutes. Sprinkle remaining cheese over top and bake for 5–15 minutes more, or until center is set.

NOTE: If you prefer, omit the onion and bell pepper and increase the amount of ham to 3 cups.

Eggs for Everybody

Makes 6 servings.

12 eggs
1 cup milk
1 cup grated Monterey
    Jack cheese, divided
1 pound bacon cooked
    and crumbled
1 bunch green onions,
    chopped

Preheat oven to 325 degrees.

In a bowl, beat together the eggs, milk, and half the cheese. Stir in the bacon and green onions. Pour mixture into a greased 9 x 13-inch pan. Cover with aluminum foil and bake for 45–55 minutes, or until eggs are set. Immediately top with remaining cheese and serve.

Southwestern Eggs

Makes 6 servings.

12 eggs
¹/₂ cup milk
2 (4-ounce) cans
    chopped green chiles
¹/₂ cup chopped red bell
    pepper
1 cup grated cheddar
    cheese
1 cup grated Monterey
    Jack cheese

Preheat oven to 350 degrees.

In a bowl, beat together the eggs and milk; set aside.

In a greased 9 x 13-inch pan, layer the chiles, bell pepper, and cheeses. Pour the egg mixture over top. Cover with aluminum foil and bake for 30–40 minutes, or until eggs are set in the center.

Omelet Brunch

Makes 6–8 servings.

18 eggs
1 cup sour cream
1 cup milk
1 teaspoon salt
1/4 cup chopped green
  onions
1 cup grated cheddar
  cheese

Preheat oven to 325 degrees.

In a large bowl, beat together the eggs, sour cream, milk, and salt. Fold in the green onions. Pour egg mixture into a greased 9 x 13-inch pan. Bake for 45–55 minutes, or until eggs are set. Immediately sprinkle cheese over top and cut into squares before serving.

Spinach Frittata

Makes 2–4 servings.

4 large eggs
1 1/2 cups milk
1/2 teaspoon salt
1 (10-ounce) package
  frozen spinach,
  thawed and drained
3/4 cup grated cheddar or
  Swiss cheese

Preheat oven to 400 degrees.

In a bowl, beat together the eggs, milk, and salt. Pour egg mixture into a greased 8 x 8-inch pan. Spread the spinach over top. Bake for 17–22 minutes, or until eggs have set. Sprinkle cheese over top and serve.

Green Chile Breakfast Casserole

Makes 6–8 *servings.*

10 eggs
1 cup cottage cheese
1/2 cup butter
1/2 cup flour
2 cups grated Colby Jack cheese
1 teaspoon baking powder
1/2 teaspoon salt
1 teaspoon garlic powder
2 (4-ounce) cans chopped green chiles
1 pound breakfast sausage, browned, and drained

Preheat oven to 350 degrees.

In a large bowl, whisk together the eggs. Add all remaining ingredients in the order listed, mixing well. Bake for about 1 hour, or until the edges are browned and a knife inserted in the center comes out clean.

Sausage–Hash Brown Breakfast Bake

Makes 6–8 *servings.*

3 1/2 cups frozen shredded hash browns

1 pound sausage, browned and drained

1 cup grated cheddar cheese

6 eggs, beaten

3/4 cup milk

1 teaspoon dry mustard

1/2 teaspoon salt

1 1/2 teaspoons black pepper

Spread the hash browns into the bottom of a greased 9 x 13-inch pan. Sprinkle cooked sausage and cheese over top.

In a bowl, combine the eggs, milk, dry mustard, salt, and pepper. Pour egg mixture evenly over sausage and hash browns. Cover and refrigerate 2 hours or overnight. Remove from refrigerator 20 minutes before baking.

Preheat oven to 350 degrees. Cover with aluminum foil and bake for 30 minutes. Uncover and bake for 5–8 minutes more, or until center is set.

Crescent, Hash Brown, and Sausage Bake

Makes 4–6 *servings.*

1 (8-ounce) tube refrigerated crescent roll dough
1 (10.4-ounce) package sausage links, browned, drained, and sliced
1 cup frozen hash browns
1 cup grated cheddar cheese
5 eggs
1⅓ cups milk
Salt and pepper, to taste
Fresh salsa

Preheat oven to 375 degrees.

Unroll the crescents and press dough over bottom and up the sides of a 12-inch round pizza pan. (Dough up the sides of the pan should have a small lip so when the egg mixture is added, it stays in the crust.) Sprinkle the sausage, hash browns, and cheese over dough.

In a bowl, beat together the eggs, milk, salt, and pepper with a fork. Pour egg mixture over dough. Bake for 30 minutes. Serve wedges with fresh salsa.

Swiss Sausage Casserole

Makes 6–8 *servings.*

10 slices white bread, cubed

1 pound spicy sausage, browned and drained

1 (4-ounce) can sliced mushrooms, drained

¾ cup grated cheddar cheese

1½ cups grated Swiss cheese

8 eggs, beaten

2 cups half-and-half

2 cups milk

¼ teaspoon salt

½ teaspoon black pepper

Place the bread cubes in a greased 9 x 13-inch pan. Crumble the sausage over bread. Evenly lay mushrooms over sausage and sprinkle cheeses over top.

In a large bowl, mix together the eggs, half-and-half, milk, salt, and pepper. Pour egg mixture evenly over cheese. Cover and refrigerate 2 hours or overnight. Remove from refrigerator 20 minutes before baking.

Preheat oven to 350 degrees. Cover with aluminum foil and bake for 30 minutes. Uncover and bake for 15–20 minutes more.

Creamy Breakfast Casserole

Makes 6–8 *servings.*

10 slices bread, crust removed, cubed

1 pound sausage, browned and drained

2 cups grated sharp cheddar cheese

6 large eggs

1 teaspoon yellow mustard

2 cups milk

1 (10.75-ounce) can cream of mushroom soup

$1/2$ cup milk

In a greased 9 x 13-inch baking dish, place the bread topped with the sausage and cheese.

In a bowl, whisk together the eggs, mustard, and 2 cups milk. Pour egg mixture over sausage. Cover and refrigerate overnight.

Preheat oven to 350 degrees. Mix together the soup and $1/2$ cup milk. Pour over bread mixture. Bake for 45 minutes.

Sausage Breakfast Casserole

Makes 4–6 servings.

1/2 pound sausage

1 teaspoon thyme

3 cups frozen shredded hash browns, thawed

6 medium eggs

1/2 cup milk

1 tablespoon dried minced onion

Salt and pepper, to taste

1 cup grated cheddar cheese

Preheat oven to 400 degrees.

Brown and drain sausage in a frying pan. Add the thyme and hash browns and set aside.

In a mixing bowl, whisk together the eggs, milk, onion, salt, and pepper. Stir in the sausage mixture and cheese. Pour into a greased 8 x 8-inch pan. Bake for 30–35 minutes, or until center is set and casserole has turned golden brown.

Sausage Grits Casserole

Makes 6–8 *servings.*

1 pound ground Italian
  pork sausage
1/2 cup chopped onion
1 teaspoon minced garlic
4 cups water
1 teaspoon salt
1 cup quick-cooking
  grits
1/2 cup milk
1/4 cup butter, softened
5 large eggs
1 1/2 cups grated cheddar
  cheese, divided

Preheat oven to 350 degrees.

In a large skillet, brown the sausage, onion, and garlic until sausage is crumbly and no longer pink; drain if necessary.

In a 3-quart saucepan, bring the water and salt to a boil. Slowly stir in the grits. Reduce heat and simmer for 4–5 minutes, stirring constantly. Remove grits from heat stir in milk and butter until butter melts.

In a 1-quart bowl, whisk the eggs until lightly beaten. Stir a spoonful of hot grits into the eggs. Quickly stir egg mixture into hot grits until eggs are completely combined. Stir in sausage mixture and 1 cup cheese. Pour grits mixture into a 9 x 13-inch pan prepared with nonstick cooking spray. Bake uncovered for 45 minutes. Sprinkle remaining cheese over top. Bake an additional 5–10 minutes.

Simple Bacon Breakfast Pie

Makes 4–6 servings.

6 medium eggs
1/2 cup milk
Salt and pepper, to taste
3 cups frozen shredded hash browns, thawed
1 cup grated Swiss cheese
1/3 cup real bacon bits

Preheat oven to 400 degrees.

In a 2-quart mixing bowl, whisk together the eggs, milk, salt, and pepper. Stir in the hash browns, cheese, and bacon. Pour mixture into a greased 8 x 8-inch pan. Bake for 30–35 minutes, or until center is set and pie has turned golden brown.

Side Dishes

Cheesy Cauliflower Bake

Makes 8-10 servings.

4 slices hearty white or wheat bread, torn into pieces
1 cup grated extra sharp cheddar cheese, divided
1 cup grated Monterey Jack cheese, divided
4 tablespoons butter, divided
4 cloves garlic, minced, divided
Salt and pepper, to taste
2 tablespoons flour
1 cup heavy cream
2/3 cup low-sodium chicken broth
2 large cauliflower heads, trimmed and cut into 3/4-inch florets (about 12 cups)
2 teaspoons dry mustard
1 teaspoon dried thyme
1/4 teaspoon salt
1/2 teaspoon pepper

Preheat the oven to 450 degrees.

In a food processor, combine the bread, 1 tablespoon cheddar cheese, 1 tablespoon Monterey Jack cheese, 1 tablespoon butter, 1 clove minced garlic, salt, and pepper and pulse until coarsely ground; set aside.

Heat the remaining butter, remaining garlic and flour in a large saucepan over medium heat, stirring constantly, about 1 minute. Slowly whisk in the cream and broth. Stir in the cauliflower, dry mustard, thyme, salt, and pepper and bring to a boil. Reduce heat to medium-low and simmer covered, stirring occasionally, until the cauliflower is nearly tender, about 6–8 minutes. Take cauliflower off the heat and stir in the remaining cheese. Pour mixture into a greased 9 x 13-inch pan and top with breadcrumb mixture. Bake until the crumbs are golden and crisp, about 10–15 minutes. Let cool 10 minutes before serving.

Simple Cauliflower Casserole

Makes 6 servings.

1 head cauliflower,
  washed and cut
  into florets
1 teaspoon lemon juice
1 (10.75-ounce) can
  cheddar cheese soup,
  condensed
$1/3$ cup mayonnaise
1 teaspoon Worcester-
  shire sauce
1 cup grated cheddar
  cheese
$1/2$ cup crumbled buttery
  round crackers

Preheat oven to 350 degrees.

In a covered saucepan, boil the cauliflower in water and lemon juice for 5 minutes until slightly tender. Drain and place cauliflower in a 2-quart casserole dish prepared with nonstick cooking spray. Gently fold in the soup, mayonnaise, Worcestershire, and cheese. Sprinkle crumbled crackers over top and then bake 30 minutes.

Baked Cheesy Zucchini

Makes 4 servings.

1 medium zucchini, thinly sliced

1 sweet onion, thinly sliced

2 Roma tomatoes, thinly sliced

2 tablespoons butter or margarine, melted

3/4 cup Italian-flavored breadcrumbs

1 cup grated mozzarella cheese

Preheat oven to 350 degrees.

In a greased 9 x 9-inch pan, layer the zucchini, onion, and tomatoes. Drizzle the butter over vegetables and then sprinkle the breadcrumbs over top. Cover and bake for 45–50 minutes, or until vegetables are tender. Remove from oven, uncover, and sprinkle cheese over top. Bake for 5–7 minutes more, or until cheese is bubbly.

Green Bean Casserole

Makes 4–6 servings.

2 (14.5-ounce) cans French-cut green beans, drained

1 (10.5-ounce) can cream of mushroom soup, condensed

2/3 cup milk

1/3 cup real bacon bits*

1/4 teaspoon black pepper

2 1/4 cups french-fried onions, divided

Preheat oven to 350 degrees.

Combine all of the ingredients except the onions in a greased 1 1/2- to 2-quart baking dish. Stir in 1 1/4 cups onions. Bake uncovered for 30 minutes, or until bubbly. Sprinkle remaining onions over top and bake 5 minutes more.

*Or about 5–7 slices of bacon, cooked and crumbled.

Asparagus Casserole

Makes 4 servings.

1 cup grated cheddar
   cheese
2 cups crushed saltine
   crackers
¼ cup butter or
   margarine, melted
1 (10.5-ounce) can
   cream of mushroom
   soup, condensed
1 (15-ounce) can
   asparagus spears,
   drained with liquid
   reserved
½ cup sliced almonds

Preheat oven to 350 degrees.

In a bowl, combine the cheese and cracker crumbs; set aside.

In a separate bowl, mix together the butter, soup, and the liquid from the can of asparagus. Layer half the cracker mixture into bottom of an 8 x 8-inch pan sprayed with nonstick spray. Arrange half the asparagus spears over top. Layer half the almonds and half the soup mixture over asparagus. Layer the remaining asparagus spears, almonds, and soup mixture over top. Cover with remaining cracker mixture. Bake for 20–25 minutes, or until bubbly and golden brown.

Yummy Baked Carrots

**4¹/₂ cups peeled and
sliced carrots**
3 tablespoons butter,
divided
¹/₂ cup chopped onion
2¹/₂ tablespoons flour
¹/₂ teaspoon salt
¹/₄ teaspoon pepper
1¹/₂ cups milk
**³/₄ cup grated cheddar
cheese**
**1 cup crushed buttery
round crackers**

Preheat oven to 350 degrees.

Cover and steam the carrots in
1¹/₂ inches of boiling water for
8 minutes; drain and set aside.

In a skillet, melt 2 tablespoons butter. Saute the onion in butter until
tender. Stir in the flour, salt, and
pepper. Gradually stir in the milk.
Stir constantly over medium heat
until the sauce bubbles and thickens. Stir in the cheese until melted.
Gently fold in the carrots.

Spoon carrot mixture into a 9 x
9-inch pan prepared with nonstick
cooking spray.

In a small microwaveable bowl,
melt the remaining butter for 15
seconds. Stir until butter is completely melted. With a fork, stir
in crushed crackers. Sprinkle the
crumb mixture evenly over top.
Bake uncovered for 30 minutes, or
until golden brown and bubbly.

Sweet Onion Casserole

Makes 6 servings.

**6 large sweet onions,
  thinly sliced**
**6 tablespoons butter or
  margarine, divided**
**1 (10.75-ounce) can
  cream of celery soup,
  condensed***
⅓ cup milk
½ teaspoon black pepper
**2 cups grated Swiss
  cheese, divided**
**6 slices French bread,
  cut 1-inch thick**

In a large frying pan, saute the onions in 4 tablespoons butter for 11–13 minutes, or until onions are tender.

Preheat oven to 350 degrees.

In a large bowl, combine the soup, milk, pepper, and 1½ cups cheese. Stir onions into the soup mixture. Spread mixture into a greased 9 x 13-inch pan. Sprinkle the remaining cheese over top. Melt remaining butter and brush it over one side of each bread slice. Place the bread slices, butter side up, in the pan making three rows. Bake for 24–28 minutes; cool 5–7 minutes before serving.

*Other varieties of condensed cream soups can be substituted.

Bacon Spinach Casserole

Makes 6 servings.

1/2 cup chopped onion
1 tablespoon olive oil
1 (10.5-ounce) can cream of golden mushroom soup, condensed
3 ounces cream cheese, softened
2 (9-ounce) packages chopped frozen spinach, thawed and drained
6-7 slices bacon, cooked and crumbled*
1/2 cup crushed seasoned croutons

Preheat oven to 350 degrees.

Saute the onion in the oil. Stir the soup and cream cheese into onion until the cream cheese melts. Stir in the spinach and bacon. Spoon mixture into a 1- to 1 1/2-quart casserole dish prepared with nonstick cooking spray. Sprinkle crushed croutons over top. Bake for 35–40 minutes, or until bubbly.

*About 1/2 cup real crumbled bacon bits or pieces can be used.

Creamy Spinach Casserole

Makes 4–6 servings.

2 (10-ounce) packages
frozen chopped
spinach
1 envelope onion soup
mix
1 (16-ounce) container
sour cream
3/4 cup grated cheddar
cheese

Preheat oven to 350 degrees.

Cook spinach according to package directions and drain. Place in a greased 1½- to 2-quart baking dish. Stir in the onion soup mix and sour cream. Sprinkle cheese over top. Bake for 20–25 minutes, or until bubbly.

Baked Cottage Cheese Mashed Potatoes

Makes 4–6 servings.

6 servings instant
mashed potatoes
1 cup cottage cheese
1 cup grated cheddar
cheese
1/4 cup chopped chives

Preheat oven to 350 degrees.

Prepare the instant mashed potatoes according to package directions. Stir in the cottage cheese, cheddar cheese, and chives. Spread the potatoes in an 8 x 8-inch pan and bake for 30–35 minutes.

Grandma's Yummy Mashed Potato Bake

Makes 6–8 *servings.*

8 medium russet potatoes
1 cup grated cheddar cheese
¼ cup butter or margarine, melted
1 (10.75-ounce) can cream of chicken soup, condensed
½ cup chopped onion
1 small jar diced pimientos, optional
1 (16-ounce) container sour cream
¾ cup crushed corn flakes or potato chips

Preheat oven to 350 degrees.

Peel and shred the potatoes. Boil shredded potatoes in water for 10 minutes and drain. Stir into the potatoes the cheese, butter, soup, onion, pimientos, and sour cream. Spread the potato mixture into a greased 9 x 13-inch pan. Bake uncovered for 45–55 minutes, or until bubbly. Sprinkle the corn flakes or chips over top and bake 5 minutes more.

Au Gratin Potato Cubes

Makes 8–10 servings.

1 (24–26-ounce) bag frozen O'Brien potatoes (cubed with peppers and onions), thawed
1/3 cup butter or margarine
2 cups half-and-half
1 teaspoon salt
1/2 teaspoon pepper
1 cup grated cheddar cheese

Preheat oven to 350 degrees.

Place the potato cubes in a lightly greased 9 x 13-inch pan and set aside.

In a saucepan, warm the butter and half-and-half over medium-low heat until butter is completely melted. Stir in the salt and pepper. Pour over potato cubes. Sprinkle cheese over top and cover with aluminum foil. Bake for 60–70 minutes, or until golden brown around the edges.

Creamy Sour Cream and Cheddar Potatoes

Makes 8–10 *servings.*

1 (24-ounce) bag frozen
O'Brien potatoes
(cubed with peppers
and onions)

1½ cups sour cream

1 (10.75-ounce) can
cream of potato
soup, condensed

1½ cups grated cheddar
cheese

⅓ cup sliced green
onion

1 cup french-fried
onions

Preheat oven to 350 degrees.

In a large bowl, mix together the potatoes, sour cream, soup, cheese, and green onion. Spread the mixture into a greased 9 x 13-inch pan. Bake uncovered for 40—50 minutes, then sprinkle french-fried onions over top. Bake for 15 minutes more or until bubbly around the edges.

Mushroom Orzo Stove Top Casserole

Makes 6–8 *servings.*

2 tablespoons butter
1/2 teaspoon minced garlic
1 1/2 cups uncooked orzo pasta
3 1/4 cups water
1 envelope onion soup mix
1 1/2 tablespoons dried parsley
8 ounces sliced mushrooms

In a 3-quart saucepan, saute the butter and garlic with the orzo over medium heat for 2 minutes, stirring constantly. Stir in the water, dry soup mix, and parsley; bring to a boil. Cover pan and reduce heat to medium low; simmer for 10 minutes. Remove lid, stir, and sprinkle sliced mushrooms evenly over top. Cover and simmer 10 minutes more. Spoon the pasta mixture into a casserole dish. Liquid will not be completely absorbed. Let stand for 5 minutes to allow liquid to absorb before serving.

Cheesy Potatoes

Makes 8–10 servings.

Preheat oven to 350 degrees.

3/4 cup Cheez Whiz
1 cup sour cream
1 (10.75-ounce) can cream of mushroom soup, condensed
1/2 cup butter or margarine, melted and divided
1 (30-ounce) package frozen shredded hash browns, thawed
1/2 cup seasoned breadcrumbs

In a large bowl, stir together the Cheez Whiz, sour cream, soup, 1/3 cup melted butter, and hash browns. Spread potato mixture evenly into a greased 9 x 13-inch pan.

In a separate bowl, mix together the breadcrumbs and remaining butter and sprinkle over top. Bake uncovered for 45–50 minutes, or until bubbly around the edges.

Corn Bread Stuffing Potatoes

Makes 8–10 *servings.*

1 (24-ounce) bag frozen cubed hash browns
2 cups sour cream
1/2 cup butter or margarine, melted
1/4 cup dry minced onion*
1 (10.75-ounce) can cream of chicken soup, condensed
1 cup grated cheddar cheese
1 (6-ounce) package seasoned corn bread stuffing mix

Preheat oven to 350 degrees.

In a large bowl, mix together all of the ingredients except the stuffing mix and spread into a greased 9 x 13-inch pan. Sprinkle the stuffing mix over top. Bake for 35–40 minutes, or until heated through and bubbly around the edges.

* 1/2 cup chopped onion can be substituted.

Potluck Potatoes

Makes 8–10 *servings.*

1 (24-ounce) bag frozen shredded hash browns

2 cups sour cream

1/2 cup butter or margarine, melted

1/2 cup chopped onion

2 (10.75-ounce) cans cream of chicken soup, condensed

1 1/2 cups grated cheddar cheese

1 1/2 cups crushed cornflakes

Preheat oven to 350 degrees.

In a large microwave-safe bowl, microwave the frozen hash browns for 4 minutes on high. Stir in the sour cream, butter, onion, soup, and cheese. Spread the mixture evenly into a greased 9 x 13-inch pan. Sprinkle the cornflakes over top. Bake uncovered for 45–50 minutes, or until bubbly around the edges.

Swiss Scalloped Potatoes

Makes 6 servings.

5–6 medium red potatoes, peeled and thinly sliced
1/2 cup sliced green onion
1 1/4 cups whipping cream or half-and-half
1 teaspoon salt
2 tablespoons butter or margarine
1 cup grated Swiss cheese

Preheat oven to 350 degrees.

Lay the potatoes in a greased 8 x 8-inch pan. Sprinkle green onion over top. Mix the cream and salt together and pour over the potatoes. Place small pieces of butter evenly over top. Cover with aluminum foil and bake for 55–65 minutes, or until potatoes are tender. Sprinkle cheese over top. Return pan to oven for 2–4 minutes more or until cheese melts.

Aunt Tammi's Scalloped Potatoes

Makes 8–10 *servings.*

5 large russet potatoes, thinly sliced
1 teaspoon salt
1/4 cup butter or margarine, melted
1 teaspoon onion powder
1/4 cup flour
2 1/2 cups milk
1 1/2 cups grated Monterey Jack or cheddar cheese

Preheat oven to 350 degrees.

Layer the potatoes in a greased 9 x 13-inch pan. Sprinkle the salt over top.

In a bowl, mix together the butter and onion powder. Whisk in the flour and milk. Pour over potatoes and stir. Bake for 60 minutes. Remove pan from oven and sprinkle cheese over top. Bake for 5–10 minutes more, or until potatoes are tender and cheese is melted.

Sweet Potato Casserole

4 1/2 pounds sweet
  potatoes
1 cup sugar
1/4 cup milk
1/2 cup butter, softened
2 large eggs
1 teaspoon vanilla
  extract
1/4 teaspoon salt
1 1/4 cups cornflakes
  cereal, crushed
1/4 cup chopped pecans
1 tablespoon brown
  sugar
1 tablespoon butter,
  melted
1 1/2 cups miniature
  marshmallows

Preheat oven to 400 degrees.

Place the potatoes on a lightly greased 15 x 10 x 1-inch pan and bake for about 1 hour, or until tender; let cool to touch and then peel and mash the potatoes. With an electric mixer, beat the mashed potatoes, sugar, milk, butter, eggs, vanilla, and salt at medium speed until smooth. Spoon the mixture into a greased 11 x 7-inch baking dish.

In a small bowl, combine the corn-flakes, pecans, brown sugar, and butter. Sprinkle the mixture diagonally over the casserole in rows 2 inches apart. Bake at 350 degrees for 30 minutes. Remove from oven; let stand 10 minutes. Sprinkle alternate rows with marshmallows; bake for 10 minutes more. Let stand 10 minutes before serving.

Chicken Rice

Makes 6–8 servings.

1 green bell pepper,
    chopped
1 medium onion,
    chopped
1 cup uncooked white
    rice
½ cup butter or
    margarine
2 (10.75-ounce each)
    cans chicken and
    rice soup, condensed
1 cup water

Preheat oven to 350 degrees.

In a frying pan, saute the bell pepper, onion, and rice in butter for about 5 minutes.

In a greased 9 x 13-inch pan, combine the rice mixture, soup, and water. Cover with aluminum foil and bake for 45–55 minutes.

Beefed-Up Pork and Beans

Makes 8–10 *servings.*

1 pound ground beef
4 (16-ounce) cans pork
   and beans
2 tablespoons mustard
1 cup ketchup
½ cup brown sugar
2 tablespoons Worces-
   tershire sauce
1 medium onion,
   chopped

Preheat oven to 400 degrees.

In a frying pan, brown the ground beef until no longer pink; drain if necessary. Combine the meat with all of the remaining ingredients in a greased 3- to 4-quart baking dish. Bake for 40–45 minutes, or until bubbly.

Supreme Pork and Beans

Makes 8–10 servings.

1 pound ground beef
1 medium onion,
    chopped
1 cup real bacon bits
1 (16-ounce) can
    garbanzo beans,
    drained and rinsed
2 (16-ounce) cans
    kidney beans,
    drained and rinsed
3 (16-ounce) cans pork
    and beans
1 cup ketchup
$1/2$ cup brown sugar
2 tablespoons yellow
    mustard
2 teaspoons white
    vinegar
$1/2$ teaspoon salt

Preheat oven to 350 degrees.

In a 6 to 8-quart size pot, brown ground beef and onion until meat is crumbly and no longer pink. Drain if necessary. Add all of the remaining ingredients into pan. Pour bean mixture into a deep-dish 9 x 13-inch pan prepared with nonstick cooking spray. Cover with aluminum foil. Bake for 45–50 minutes, until bubbly. Serve with corn bread muffins.

Cilantro Spanish Rice

Makes 6 servings

1 medium onion,
  chopped
1 teaspoon minced garlic
2 tablespoons olive oil
1 (15-ounce) can black
  beans, rinsed and
  drained
1 (15-ounce) can whole
  kernel corn, drained
1 (10.75-ounce) can
  tomato soup,
  condensed
1$\frac{1}{4}$ cups water
1 cup uncooked instant
  rice
1$\frac{1}{2}$ teaspoons chili
  powder
2 teaspoons dried
  cilantro
$\frac{1}{2}$ teaspoon cumin
$\frac{1}{2}$ teaspoon salt
$\frac{1}{4}$ teaspoon pepper

Preheat oven to 350 degrees.

In 4-quart pan, saute onion and garlic in olive oil until tender. Stir in all the remaining ingredients. Pour the mixture into a 9 x 9-inch pan prepared with nonstick cooking spray. Cover with aluminum foil and bake for 35 minutes. Stir and serve as a side to your favorite Mexican main dish.

Vegetable
Dishes

Parmesan Veggie Frittata

Makes 6 servings.

2 tablespoons olive oil
1/2 cup chopped onion
2 teaspoons jarred minced garlic
1/2 red or orange bell pepper, diced
1 (10-ounce) box frozen chopped spinach, thawed
8 large eggs
Salt and pepper, to taste
1/2 cup milk
3/4 cup grated Parmesan cheese
1/2 cup crumbled feta cheese

Preheat oven to 375 degrees.

Preheat oil in a 9 x 9-inch baking pan for 10 minutes. Sprinkle the onion, garlic, and bell pepper evenly over pan.

Use paper towels to squeeze dry the thawed spinach. Add the spinach evenly over the vegetables.

In a 2-quart bowl, whisk together the eggs, salt, pepper, and milk until smooth. Whisk in the Parmesan cheese. Pour egg mixture evenly over spinach mixture. Sprinkle feta cheese over top. Bake for 35–40 minutes, or until golden brown and set in the center.

Layered Potato, Tomato, and Bell Pepper Casserole

Makes 4 servings.

4 medium potatoes,
    peeled
4 Roma tomatoes, sliced
1 large green bell
    pepper, seeded and
    cut into strips
Salt and pepper, to taste
1 teaspoon Italian
    seasoning
2 cups grated mozzarella
    cheese
1 cup sour cream

Preheat oven to 400 degrees.

In a stockpot, boil the potatoes for 25–30 minutes, until partially cooked, and then thinly slice. Layer half each of the potato slices, tomato slices, and bell pepper strips in a greased 9 x 9-inch pan. Season with salt and pepper. Sprinkle half each of the Italian seasoning and mozzarella cheese over the vegetables. Repeat layers with remaining potatoes, tomatoes, and bell pepper. Sprinkle remaining seasoning and cheese over vegetables and then spread sour cream over top. Cover and bake for 30–40 minutes, or until bubbly.

Butternut Squash Lasagna

Makes 6–8 servings.

1 cup chopped onion
3–4 cups fresh spinach
   leaves
1½ cups grated
   mozzarella cheese
Salt and pepper, to taste
2 eggs
1 (16-ounce) container
   cottage cheese,
   drained well
1½ cups butternut
   squash, peeled
   and diced
1 (26-ounce) jar
   spaghetti sauce
1 package oven-ready
   lasagna noodles
½ cup grated Parmesan
   cheese

Preheat oven to 375 degrees.

Heat a large skillet coated with cooking spray over medium-high heat. Add the onion and saute until tender. Add the spinach and continue cooking for about a minute, or until spinach wilts. Combine the mozzarella, salt, pepper, eggs, and cottage cheese in a large bowl; set aside.

Place the squash in a microwave-safe bowl and microwave on high for 5 minutes, or until squash becomes tender.

In the bottom of a greased 9 x 13-inch baking dish, spread a little of the spaghetti sauce and arrange 3 noodles over top. Spread half of the cheese mixture over the noodles. Arrange the squash over cheese mixture. Spread a third of the spaghetti sauce over the squash. Place 3 noodles over sauce and spread remaining cheese mixture over the noodles. Arrange the spinach mixture over the cheese mixture and a third of the sauce over the spinach. Arrange

3 noodles over sauce; spread remaining sauce evenly over noodles. Sprinkle with the Parmesan. Bake covered with aluminum foil for 30 minutes. Uncover and bake an additional 30 minutes.

Veggie Shepherd's Pie

Makes 4 servings.

1 (16-ounce) bag frozen California-blend vegetables
1 (10.75-ounce) can cheddar cheese soup, condensed
1½ teaspoons thyme
2 cups mashed potatoes, seasoned with garlic

Preheat oven to 350 degrees.

In a greased 9 x 9-inch pan, combine the frozen vegetables, soup, and thyme. Spread the potatoes evenly over the vegetable layer. Cover and bake for 25 minutes. Uncover and bake for 15–20 minutes more, or until heated through.

Chive 'n' Potato Casserole

Makes 6-8 servings.

Preheat oven to 350 degrees.

4 cups mashed potatoes
1 cup sour cream
1 (8-ounce) package
   cream cheese,
   softened
1 tablespoon chives
1/2 teaspoon garlic
   powder
1/3 cup breadcrumbs
1 tablespoon butter or
   margarine, melted

In a large bowl, combine the potatoes, sour cream, cream cheese, chives, and garlic powder. Spread mixture into a greased 2-quart casserole dish. Sprinkle the breadcrumbs over potatoes and then drizzle the butter over top. Bake for 50 minutes.

Cheesy Rice and Veggie Bake

Makes 6–8 servings.

2 cups water
1 cup uncooked white rice
1 (16-ounce) bag frozen broccoli florets
1 (16-ounce) bag frozen cauliflower florets
1⅓ cups water
1 medium onion, chopped
⅓ cup butter or margarine
1 (16-ounce) jar Cheez Whiz
1 (10.75-ounce) can cream of celery soup, condensed
⅔ cup milk

In a saucepan, bring the water and rice to a boil; reduce heat. Cover and simmer for 15 minutes, or until water is absorbed.

In a bowl, heat the broccoli and cauliflower with 1⅓ cup water in a microwave on high heat for 8 minutes, or until tender; drain vegetables.

Preheat oven to 350 degrees.

In a frying pan, saute the onion in the butter. Stir in the cooked rice. Spread rice mixture into a greased 9 x 13-inch pan. Stir the vegetables, cheese sauce, soup, and milk into rice mixture. Bake for 30–35 minutes, or until bubbly.

Summer Garden Corn Bread Casserole

Makes 6 servings.

1 (8.5-ounce) box corn muffin mix

2–3 medium yellow summer squash, peeled and cubed

¼ cup butter

1 (10.75-ounce) can cream of mushroom soup, condensed

1 cup plain yogurt

1 tablespoon sugar

1 green bell pepper, chopped

1 medium onion, chopped

Salt and pepper, to taste

Bake the corn bread according to package directions in a greased 8 x 8-inch pan; set aside to cool.

Preheat oven to 375 degrees.

Boil the squash in salted water for 3–5 minutes, or until tender; drain. Stir in the butter until melted.

In a large bowl, combine the buttered squash and remaining ingredients. Crumble the corn bread and fold it into squash mixture. Place mixture into a 2-quart casserole dish prepared with nonstick cooking spray. Bake for 35–40 minutes, or until golden brown.

Vegetable Stuffing Casserole

Makes 7–9 servings.

1 (16-ounce) bag frozen
   green beans
1 (16-ounce) bag frozen
   mixed vegetables
2 (10.75-ounce) cans
   cream of mushroom
   soup, condensed
1 (6-ounce) can french-
   fried onions
1 (6-ounce) box seasoned
   stuffing mix
3 tablespoons butter or
   margarine, melted
¼ cup water

Preheat oven to 350 degrees.

Pour the frozen vegetables into the bottom of a greased 9 x 13-inch pan. Stir the soup into the vegetables. Sprinkle the onions and stuffing mix evenly over top. Drizzle the butter and water over the stuffing layer. Cover with aluminum foil and bake for 55–65 minutes, or until heated through.

Corn Lover's Casserole

Makes 4–6 servings.

2 eggs, slightly beaten
1 (14.75-ounce) can
    cream style corn
1 (12-ounce) can whole
    kernel corn, drained
3/4 cup sour cream
3 tablespoons butter or
    margarine, melted
1 1/2 cups grated cheddar
    cheese
1 medium onion,
    chopped
1 (4-ounce) can chopped
    green chiles, drained
1 (6.5-ounce) package
    corn muffin mix

Preheat oven to 350 degrees.

In a large bowl, combine the eggs, corn, sour cream, butter, cheese, onion, and chiles. Gently fold in the corn muffin mix until moistened. Spread mixture into a greased 2-quart baking dish. Bake for 60–70 minutes, or until golden brown on top and the center is set.

Stacked Black Bean Tortilla Pie

Makes 4–5 *servings.*

1 (16-ounce) can refried
   beans
1 cup salsa, divided
1 teaspoon minced garlic
1 tablespoon dried
   cilantro
1 (15-ounce) can black
   beans, rinsed and
   drained
1 medium tomato,
   chopped
7 medium flour tortillas
2 cups grated cheddar
   cheese
Salsa, for garnish
Sour cream, for garnish

Preheat oven to 400 degrees.

In a bowl, combine the refried beans, $^3/_4$ cup salsa, and garlic.

In a separate bowl, combine the remaining salsa, cilantro, black beans, and tomato. Place a tortilla in the bottom of a greased pie pan. Spread a fourth of the refried bean mixture over tortilla within $^1/_2$ inch of the edge. Sprinkle $^1/_4$ cup cheese over beans and cover with another tortilla. Spoon a third of the black bean mixture over tortilla. Sprinkle $^1/_4$ cup cheese over black bean mixture and cover with another tortilla. Repeat layers, ending with a final layer of retried bean mixture spread over the last tortilla. Sprinkle with $^1/_2$ cup cheese. Cover and bake for 35–40 minutes. Serve individual pieces of pie with salsa and sour cream.

Tortilla and Black Bean Casserole

Makes 6–8 servings.

1 onion, chopped
2 (10-ounce) cans tomatoes with green chiles
1 cup picante sauce
1 teaspoon ground cumin
2 (15-ounce) cans black beans, drained and rinsed
4 ounces reduced-fat cream cheese
10 (7-inch) corn tortillas (flour tortillas also work)
2 cups grated Monterey Jack cheese
Sour cream, for garnish
Guacamole, for garnish
Shredded lettuce, for garnish

Preheat oven to 350 degrees.

In large skillet, sauté the onion until soft. Add the tomatoes, picante sauce, and cumin and bring to a boil. Reduce heat and simmer 10 minutes. Stir in the beans and heat thoroughly. Add the cream cheese and stir until melted; remove from heat. Spray the bottom of a 9 x 13-inch pan with cooking spray. Spread a third of the bean mixture on bottom of pan, topping with a layer of tortillas and half the cheese. Repeat layers. Sprinkle remaining cheese on top. Cover with aluminum foil and bake for 20–25 minutes. Uncover and bake for 10 minutes more. Let stand for 5–10 minutes before serving. Serve garnished with sour cream, lettuce, and guacamole as desired.

Layered Mexican Pizza

Makes 5–7 servings.

1 (13.8-ounce) tube
    refrigerated pizza
    crust dough
1 (16-ounce) can refried
    beans
³/₄ cup chunky salsa
1 envelope taco
    seasoning
1¹/₂ cups grated Mexican-
    blend cheese
1 (10-ounce) bag
    shredded lettuce
2 Roma tomatoes, diced
1¹/₂ cups crushed nacho
    cheese tortilla chips

Preheat oven to 400 degrees.

Cover the bottom and partially up the sides of a greased 9 x 13-inch pan with pizza dough. Bake for 10–12 minutes, or until light golden brown.

In a saucepan, heat the refried beans and salsa together until bubbly. Stir taco seasoning into refried bean mixture. Spread the bean mixture over the baked crust. Sprinkle cheese over beans and bake for 5–8 minutes, or until cheese is melted. Layer the lettuce, tomatoes, and crushed chips over top and serve immediately.

Rice and Green Chile Casserole

Makes 4–6 *servings.*

1 (6-ounce) box instant long grain and wild rice mix

1 cup sour cream

1 (4-ounce) can chopped green chiles, drained

1 cup grated cheddar cheese

1 cup grated Monterey Jack cheese

Prepare rice according to package directions; set aside.

Preheat oven to 350 degrees.

In a bowl, mix together the sour cream and green chiles. Spread half the cooked rice over the bottom of a greased 8 x 8-inch pan. Spoon half the sour cream mixture over the rice. Sprinkle half of each cheese over top. Spoon remaining rice over cheese. Spread the remaining sour cream mixture over rice, sprinkle remaining cheese over top. Bake uncovered for 15–20 minutes, or until bubbly.

Creamy Hominy Bake

Makes 4–5 *servings.*

1 medium onion,
    chopped
1 large green bell
    pepper, seeded
    and diced
$1/2$ cup butter or
    margarine
1 (15.5-ounce) can white
    hominy, drained
1 (15.5-ounce) can
    yellow hominy,
    drained
1 (12-ounce) can whole
    kernel corn, drained
1 (4-ounce) can sliced
    mushrooms, drained
$1/4$ cup grated Parmesan
    cheese
1 cup Cheez Whiz
$1/4$ cup diced pimiento,
    drained

Preheat oven to 350 degrees.

In a frying pan, saute the onion and bell pepper in the butter until tender. Stir remaining ingredients into onion mixture. Spread into a greased 8 x 8-inch pan. Bake for 30–35 minutes, or until bubbly.

Beef Dishes

Beef and Potato Pie

1½ pounds ground beef
2 large potatoes, peeled
   and cubed
Salt and pepper, to taste
1 (16-ounce) container
   cottage cheese
2 eggs
½ cup sour cream
1 teaspoon oregano
2 deep-dish pie shells
2 cups grated cheddar
   cheese

In a frying pan, brown the ground beef until no longer pink; drain if necessary and set aside.

In a pot, boil the potatoes in salted water until tender; drain, mash, and season the potatoes with salt and pepper.

In a blender, blend together the cottage cheese, eggs, sour cream, and oregano until smooth. Stir the mixture into potatoes. Divide the ground beef between the pie shells. Spread the potato mixture evenly over the ground beef. Sprinkle the cheese over top. Bake for 30–35 minutes and serve.

Meat Pies

Makes 4–6 servings.

1 pound ground beef
1 small onion, minced
1 egg, slightly beaten
$^1/_2$ cup fine dry
   breadcrumbs
1 tablespoon ketchup
$^1/_2$ teaspoon
   Worcestershire sauce
1 teaspoon salt
$^1/_4$ teaspoon pepper
1 (15-ounce) package
   refrigerated pie
   crusts

Preheat oven to 400 degrees.

In a large frying pan, brown the ground beef with onion until meat is no longer pink and onion is transparent; drain if necessary and set aside.

In a bowl, combine the egg, breadcrumbs, ketchup, Worcestershire sauce, salt, and pepper. Pour mixture into meat then heat through and set aside.

Lay 1 crust in a deep-dish pie pan. Spoon beef mixture into pie shell. Cover with remaining crust and seal the edges. Cut a few slits in the top crust to allow steam to vent during baking. Bake for 23–28 minutes, or until golden brown. Let stand for 5 minutes before serving.

Asparagus Shepherd's Pie

Makes 4-6 servings.

1 pound ground beef

1 medium onion, chopped

1 teaspoon minced garlic

1 (14.75-ounce) can cream of asparagus soup

1 (15-ounce) can asparagus, drained

4 cups mashed potatoes

Preheat oven to 350 degrees.

In a frying pan, brown the ground beef, onion, and garlic until the meat is no longer pink; drain if necessary. Combine beef with soup. Spread the mixture into the bottom of a greased 8 x 8- or 9 x 9-inch pan. Lay asparagus evenly over meat mixture. Spread mashed potatoes evenly over asparagus. Bake uncovered for 15–20 minutes, or until thoroughly heated.

Creamy Mushroom Shepherd's Pie

Makes 4 servings.

1 pound ground beef or
  turkey
¼ cup chopped onion
1 (4-ounce) can
  mushroom pieces,
  drained
1 (14.5-ounce) can green
  beans, drained
1 (10.75-ounce) can
  cream of mushroom
  soup, condensed
4 cups mashed potatoes

Preheat oven to 350 degrees.

In a frying pan, brown the beef with the onion and drain if necessary. Stir in the mushrooms, green beans, and soup. Spread mixture in a greased 8 x 8-inch or 9 x 9-inch pan. Spoon the potatoes evenly over top. Bake uncovered for 20–25 minutes, or until hot in the center and bubbly around the edges.

Cabbage and Beef Pot Pie

Preheat oven to 375 degrees.

1 pound ground beef
1 medium onion, chopped
1 (16-ounce) bag shredded cabbage and carrot coleslaw blend
2¼ cups water, divided
2 (.87-ounce) envelopes brown gravy mix
2 frozen ready-to-bake pie crusts, thawed

In a large frying pan, brown the ground beef and onion until no longer pink; drain if necessary. Add the coleslaw and 1 cup water. Cover and simmer over low heat, stirring occasionally, until vegetables are almost done. Stir in the gravy mix and remaining water. Simmer until gravy thickens. Lay 1 crust in a deep-dish pie pan. Spoon beef mixture into pie shell. Cover with remaining crust and seal the edges. Cut a few slits in the top crust to allow steam to vent during baking. Bake for 23–28 minutes, or until golden brown. Let stand for 5 minutes before serving.

Beef Pot Pie

Makes 6–8 servings.

1 pound lean beef stew
   meat, cooked
1 (16-ounce) package
   frozen mixed
   vegetables, thawed
1 (12-ounce) jar
   mushroom gravy
$1/2$ teaspoon thyme
1 (8-ounce) tube
   refrigerated
   crescent rolls

Preheat oven to 375 degrees.

Combine all of the ingredients except the rolls in a greased 9 x 13-inch pan. Bake for 20 minutes. Remove from oven and place flattened dough over top. Return to oven and bake 17–19 minutes more, or until crust is golden brown.

Easy Cheeseburger Pie

Makes 4 servings.

1 pound ground beef,
   browned and drained
1 cup chopped onion
1 cup grated cheddar
   cheese
1 cup milk
$1/2$ cup biscuit mix
2 eggs

Preheat oven to 325 degrees.

In a greased 9 x 9-inch pan, layer the beef, onion, and cheese. In a bowl, combine the milk, biscuit mix, and eggs. Spread the dough mixture over top. Bake for 25–35 minutes, or until knife inserted in the center comes out clean.

Sloppy Joe Pie

Makes 4–6 servings.

Preheat oven to 375 degrees.

1 pound ground beef
1 medium onion,
   chopped
1 (15-ounce) can
   crushed tomatoes,
   with liquid
1 envelope sloppy joe
   seasoning mix
1 (8-ounce) tube
   refrigerated
   crescent roll dough

In a frying pan, brown the beef and onion together until beef is done. Stir in the tomatoes and seasoning. Simmer over medium-low heat for 5 minutes, stirring occasionally. Place the mixture into a greased, deep 9-inch pie pan or round baking dish. Lay individually the flattened crescents over top, placing the skinny point in the center, stretching the bottom edge of the crescent dough triangle to the outside of the pan. Overlap dough if necessary. Bake for 15 minutes, or until crust is golden brown.

Incredible Cheeseburger Casserole

Makes 6–8 servings.

2 pounds ground beef
1 large onion, chopped
1 (10-ounce) can
   tomatoes with
   green chiles
1/2 teaspoon salt
1/2 teaspoon black
   pepper
1 3/4 cups grated sharp
   cheddar cheese
1 cup biscuit mix
1 3/4 cups milk
3 eggs, lightly beaten
Shredded lettuce
Salsa

Preheat oven to 400 degrees.

In a frying pan, brown the beef and onion and drain any excess grease. Stir in the diced tomatoes and chiles, salt and pepper. Spread the mixture into a greased 9 x 13-inch pan and sprinkle the cheese over top.

In a bowl, mix together the biscuit mix, milk, and eggs. Pour batter over top. Bake for 25–30 minutes, or until lightly golden brown and set in the center. Serve individual pieces topped with desired amount of shredded lettuce and salsa.

Meat and Potato Casserole

Makes 6–8 *servings.*

Preheat oven to 350 degrees

1 pound ground beef
2 medium onions,
chopped
1½ teaspoons Italian
seasoning
4–6 medium potatoes,
peeled and thinly
sliced
Salt and pepper, to taste
1 (10.75-ounce) can
cream of mushroom
soup, condensed
⅓ cup water

In a frying pan, brown the beef and onion together until beef is done. Stir in the Italian seasoning, lay a third of the potato slices on the bottom of a greased 9 x 13-inch pan. Sprinkle the potatoes with salt and pepper. Spread half the beef mixture over top. Repeat layers, ending with potato layer. Combine the soup and water and pour the mixture over top. Cover with aluminum foil and bake for 1 hour.

Creamy Beef, Pea, and Potato Casserole

Makes 8 *servings.*

1 (26-ounce) bag frozen
    shredded hash
    browns
1 pound ground beef,
    browned and drained
1/2 cup chopped onion
1 1/2 cups frozen peas
2 cups half-and-half or
    milk
2 (10.75-ounce) cans
    cream of chicken
    soup, condensed
1 cup grated cheddar
    cheese

Preheat oven to 350 degrees.

Place the hash browns in the bottom of a greased 9 x 13-inch pan. Spread the beef and onion over the hash browns. Sprinkle the peas over top and set aside.

In a mixing bowl, combine the half-and-half and soup. Pour over casserole. Sprinkle the cheese over top and bake for 60–70 minutes, or until golden brown and bubbly around the edges.

Summer Zucchini Casserole

Makes 6–8 *servings.*

2 cups sliced zucchini
1/4 cup chopped onion
1 (10.75-ounce) can
　　cream of chicken
　　soup
1 cup sour cream
1 cup grated carrots
1 pound ground beef,
　　browned and drained
1/2 cup unsalted butter,
　　melted
1 (6-ounce) box chicken-
　　flavored stuffing mix

Preheat oven to 350 degrees.

Boil the zucchini and onion in water for 5 minutes; drain well and set aside.

In a medium bowl, combine the soup, sour cream, and carrots. Stir in the zucchini, onion, and browned ground beef.

In a separate bowl, combine the butter and stuffing mix, stirring until stuffing is well coated with butter. Spread half the stuffing mix on the bottom of a greased 9 x 13-inch baking dish. Spoon the zucchini mixture over the stuffing and then top with the remaining stuffing mix. Bake for 25–30 minutes, or until stuffing is golden brown.

Tater Tot Casserole

Makes 6–8 *servings.*

1 pound ground beef
1 medium onion,
    chopped
2 (10.75-ounce) cans
    cream of mushroom
    or chicken soup,
    condensed
1 (15-ounce) can whole
    kernel corn, drained
1 cup grated cheddar
    cheese
1 (27–32-ounce) bag
    frozen tater tots

Preheat oven to 350 degrees.

In a frying pan, brown the beef and onion together until beef is done; drain if necessary. Place the mixture into the bottom of a greased 9 x 13-inch pan. Spoon 1 can soup over top. Sprinkle the corn and cheese over the soup layer. Cover with tater tots, laying them sideways. Spread the remaining soup over top and bake for 40 minutes.

Beef and Scalloped Potatoes

Makes 8 servings.

5–6 large russet potatoes, sliced (about 2 1/2 pounds)

1 cup chopped onion, divided

2 teaspoons salt, divided

1 cup grated Swiss or cheddar cheese

1 1/2 pounds ground beef

3/4 cup sour cream

1/2 cup crushed saltine crackers

Preheat oven to 350 degrees.

Layer the potatoes, 3/4 cup onion, 1 teaspoon salt, and cheese evenly in a greased 9 x 13-inch pan.

In a separate bowl, mix together the beef, sour cream, saltines, remaining onion, and remaining salt. Place the beef mixture over the potato mixture. Bake covered with aluminum foil for 30 minutes. Remove foil and bake for 20 minutes more, or until meat and potatoes are done.

Buried Cube Steaks

Makes 4–6 servings.

**4 cube steaks (about
    1 pound)**
Salt and pepper, to taste
**4–5 Yukon Gold
    potatoes, peeled and
    thinly sliced**
**1 medium sweet onion,
    thinly sliced**
**2 (10.75-ounce) cans
    cream of mushroom
    soup, condensed**

Preheat oven to 350 degrees.

Place the cube steaks in the bottom of a lightly greased 9 x 13-inch pan. Add the salt and pepper. Layer the potatoes and onion over the steaks. Spread the soup over top. Cover with aluminum foil and bake for 70–75 minutes, or until meat is done.

Onion Ring Barbecue Bake

Makes 6–8 servings.

1½ pounds ground beef
**1 medium onion,
    chopped**
**1 (18-ounce) bottle
    hickory barbecue
    sauce**
**1 (16-ounce) bag frozen
    onion rings**

Preheat oven to 425 degrees.

In a frying pan, brown the beef and onion together until beef is done; drain if necessary. Stir the barbecue sauce into the beef and onion. Spread the mixture into a greased 9 x 13-inch pan. Place onion rings evenly over top. Bake for 20–25 minutes, or until the onion rings are crisp.

Saucy Meat and Potatoes

Makes 4–6 servings.

Preheat oven to 350 degrees.

5–6 medium red potatoes, peeled and thinly sliced

¾ cup steak sauce, divided

2 pounds ground beef

¾ cup seasoned breadcrumbs

⅔ cup chopped onion

Lay the potato slices on the bottom of a greased 8 x 8-inch or 9 x 9-inch pan.

In a large bowl, combine ¼ cup steak sauce, beef, breadcrumbs, and onion. Press the mixture evenly over the potato layer. Spread remaining steak sauce over top. Bake uncovered for 65–75 minutes, or until beef is completely cooked through.

Cowboy Casserole

1 pound ground beef
1 medium onion,
    chopped
2 jalapeño peppers,
    seeded and diced
2 (6.5-ounce) packages
    corn bread mix
1/2 teaspoon salt
1 1/2 teaspoons baking
    soda
1 (14.75-ounce) can
    cream style corn
3/4 cup milk
2 eggs, beaten
2 cups grated cheddar
    cheese, divided

Preheat oven to 350 degrees.

In a frying pan, brown the beef with the onion and peppers until beef is done; drain if necessary and set aside.

In a bowl, combine the corn bread mix, salt, baking soda, corn, milk, and eggs. Spread half the batter over the bottom of a greased 9 x 13-inch pan. Sprinkle half the cheese over batter. Spoon meat mixture evenly over top. Sprinkle remaining cheese over meat mixture, and then spread remaining batter over top. Bake uncovered for 35 minutes, or until corn bread is golden brown and set in the center.

Corn Bread Topped Chili

Makes 6–8 servings.

Preheat oven to 425 degrees.

1 medium onion,
chopped
1 tablespoon butter or
margarine
2 (15-ounce) cans chili
with meat and beans
1 (11-ounce) can
Mexican-style corn,
drained
1 cup grated cheddar
cheese
1 (8.5-ounce) package
corn bread mix

In a frying pan, saute the onion in butter until tender. Stir in the chili and corn. Spread the mixture into a greased 9 x 13-inch pan. Sprinkle the cheese over top.

In a bowl, mix the corn bread mix according to package directions. Pour batter evenly over the chili mixture. Bake for 25 minutes, or until corn bread is golden brown and set in the center.

Chili Casserole

Makes 6 servings.

Preheat oven to 350 degrees.

1 (14-ounce) bag tortilla chips, crushed
2 (15-ounce) cans chili con carne
1 (8-ounce) can tomato sauce
2 cups grated cheddar cheese

Sprinkle half the chips over the bottom of a 9 x 13-inch glass pan. Spread 1 can chili over the chip layer. Drizzle half the tomato sauce over top. Sprinkle 1 cup cheese over sauce. Repeat layers. Bake for 17–22 minutes, until heated through. Serve with salsa on the side if desired.

Empanada Pie

Makes 8 servings.

Preheat oven to 400 degrees.

1 pound ground beef
2 onions, chopped
2 teaspoons paprika
1 teaspoon cumin
1 teaspoon salt
1/3 cup raisins
1/2 cup sliced black olives
2 refrigerated 9-inch pie crusts

In a pan, brown the ground beef and onions until meat is no longer pink. Stir in the paprika, cumin, and salt; remove from heat. Stir in the raisins and olives. Lay 1 crust in a deep-dish pie pan. Spoon the meat mixture into the crust. Lay second crust over top and seal edges by pinching together. Cut four slits in top crust to allow steam to escape. Bake for 30 minutes, or until golden.

Southwest Casserole

Preheat oven to 350 degrees.

1 pound ground beef, browned and drained

2 (8-ounce) cans tomato sauce

1 (15-ounce) can whole kernel corn, drained

1 envelope taco seasoning

10 medium gordita-style flour tortillas

1 (10.75-ounce) can cream of celery soup, condensed

3/4 cup milk

1 1/2 cups grated cheddar or Mexican-blend cheese

In a bowl, combine the beef, tomato sauce, corn, and taco seasoning. Use 6 tortillas to cover the bottom and sides of a greased 9 x 13-inch pan. Spread the mixture over the tortillas. Use the remaining tortillas to cover the beef mixture, cutting to fit if necessary. Mix together the soup and milk and pour over tortillas. Sprinkle the cheese over top. Bake for 20–25 minutes, or until edges turn golden brown.

Enchilada Casserole

Makes 6 servings.

1 pound ground beef,
   browned and drained
1 (15-ounce) can chili,
   any variety
1 (8-ounce) can tomato
   sauce
1 (10-ounce) can
   enchilada sauce
1 (10-ounce) bag Fritos
   corn chips, divided
1 cup sour cream
1 cup grated cheddar
   cheese

Preheat oven to 350 degrees.

In a large bowl, combine the beef, chili, tomato sauce, and enchilada sauce. Stir in two-thirds of the chips. Spread mixture into a greased 2-quart baking dish. Bake uncovered for 24–28 minutes, or until heated through. Spread the sour cream over top. Sprinkle cheese over sour cream. Crush remaining chips and sprinkle over top. Bake for 5–8 minutes more, or until cheese is melted.

Cream Cheese Enchiladas

Makes 6–8 *servings.*

Preheat oven to 375 degrees.

1 pound ground beef,
    browned and drained
1/2 cup chopped onion
2 (8-ounce) cans tomato
    sauce
1/4 cup water
1 1/2 teaspoons chili
    powder
1 1/2 teaspoons black
    pepper
1 (8-ounce) package
    cream cheese,
    softened
12 medium flour tortillas
2 cups grated cheddar
    cheese
Shredded lettuce
Sour cream

In a large bowl, combine the beef, onion, tomato sauce, water, and spices. Spread the cream cheese down the center of each tortilla, roll up, and place in a greased 9 x 13-inch pan. Pour beef mixture over top and sprinkle with the cheese. Cover with aluminum foil and bake for 25 minutes. Uncover and bake an additional 5 minutes, or until cheese is melted and golden brown. Serve over shredded lettuce and top with a dollop of sour cream.

Deep-Dish Tacos

Makes 4 *servings.*

1/2 cup sour cream
1/2 cup mayonnaise
1/2 cup grated cheddar
   cheese
1/4 cup chopped onion
1 cup biscuit mix
1/4 cup cold water
1/2 pound ground beef,
   browned and drained
1 medium tomato, thinly
   sliced
1/2 cup chopped green
   bell pepper

Preheat oven to 375 degrees.

In a bowl, combine the sour cream, mayonnaise, cheese, and onion; set aside.

In a separate bowl, mix biscuit mix and water until a soft dough forms. Press dough on bottom and up the sides of a greased 8 x 8-inch pan. Layer the beef, tomato, and bell pepper over dough. Spoon sour cream mixture over top. Bake for 25–30 minutes.

Creamy Tortilla Pie

Makes 6 – 8 *servings.*

1 pound ground beef
1 medium onion,
    chopped
1 (4-ounce) can diced
    green chiles, with
    liquid
2 (8-ounce) cans tomato
    sauce
1 envelope taco
    seasoning
4 large flour tortillas
¾ cup milk
1 (10.75-ounce) can
    cream of chicken
    soup, condensed
2 cups grated cheddar
    cheese, divided

Preheat oven to 350 degrees.

In a frying pan, brown the ground beef and onion until meat is no longer pink; drain if necessary. Stir in the green chiles, tomato sauce, and taco seasoning. Center 2 large tortillas over two greased pie pans. Press tortillas down to form a bottom crust. Evenly divide meat mixture between pans. Lay the remaining tortillas over tops, cutting to fit if necessary.

In a bowl, combine the milk and soup. Pour half the soup mixture evenly over each pie. Sprinkle 1 cup cheese over each. Cover with aluminum foil and bake for 15 minutes. Uncover and bake for 5 minutes more, or until cheese melts.

NOTE: You can freeze a pie to be used at a later date. To bake after freezing, place the pie in the refrigerator 24 hours before baking. Bake thawed pie, covered in aluminum foil, at 350 degrees for 20 minutes. Uncover and bake 5 minutes more, or until cheese melts.

Mashed Potato Taco Pie

Makes 4 *servings.*

1 pound ground beef,
  browned and drained
1 envelope taco
  seasoning
1 (8-ounce) can tomato
  sauce
1 (15-ounce) can whole
  kernel corn, drained
1 (14.75-ounce) can
  cream style corn
4 cups mashed potatoes

Preheat oven to 350 degrees.

In a bowl, combine the beef, taco seasoning, and tomato sauce. Layer the beef mixture, corn, and potatoes in a greased 8 x 8-inch or 9 x 9-inch pan. Bake uncovered for 20–25 minutes, or until hot in the center and bubbly around the edges.

Quick Mexican Dinner

Makes 4–6 *servings.*

1 pound ground beef,
  browned and drained
1 (15.5-ounce) can
  sloppy joe sauce
1 (11-ounce) can
  Mexican-style corn
2 cups grated pepper
  jack cheese
1 (6-ounce) tube
  refrigerated biscuits

Preheat oven to 375 degrees.

Combine the beef, sloppy joe sauce, and corn. Layer the beef mixture in the bottom of a 9 x 9-inch pan. Sprinkle cheese over top. Cut biscuits in half and lay over the cheese cut side down. Bake for 15–20 minutes, until heated through and biscuits are golden.

Cheesy Mexican Casserole

Makes 8–10 servings.

2 pounds ground beef
1/2 small onion, diced
1 (10-ounce) can
   tomatoes with
   green chiles
1 envelope taco
   seasoning
1 (8-ounce) box Mexican
   Velveeta cheese,
   diced
2 (8-count) tubes
   refrigerated
   crescent rolls
Garnishes: lettuce,
   tomatoes, sour
   cream, olives, and
   jalapeños

Preheat oven to 400 degrees.

Brown the ground beef with the onion and drain well. Combine the beef and onion with of the tomatoes, taco seasoning, and cheese. Press 1 can crescent rolls into the bottom of lightly greased 9 x 13-inch pan to cover completely. Layer the beef mixture on top of the dough and place remaining crescent rolls over top to cover completely. Bake for 15–20 minutes. Add garnishes as desired.

Taco Layer Dip

Makes 8–10 *servings.*

1 (8-ounce) package
   cream cheese
1 (15-ounce) can no
   bean beef chili
1 (4-ounce) can green
   chilies, drained
1 (2.25-ounce) can sliced
   black olives, drained
¼ cup sliced green
   onions
⅔ cup Mexican-blend
   cheese
Tortilla chips

Preheat oven to 350 degrees.

Spread cream cheese into the bottom of 9-inch pie pan. Spoon chili and green chilies evenly over top cream cheese layer. Sprinkle black olives, green onions, and cheese evenly over top. Bake uncovered for 30 minutes, until bubbly and cheese is melted. Serve with tortilla chips.

Chilean Corn Casserole

Makes 6–8 *servings.*

4 (15-ounce) cans whole
    kernel corn, drained
1¹⁄₂ teaspoons basil
1 teaspoon salt
3 tablespoons butter or
    margarine
1 tablespoon cornstarch
1¹⁄₂ pounds ground beef
3 large onions, chopped
1 teaspoon ground cumin
1 (2.25-ounce) can
    sliced black olives,
    drained
¹⁄₂ cup raisins
2 tablespoons sugar

Preheat oven to 400 degrees.

In a blender, puree the corn for 3 minutes. Pour the liquefied corn into a saucepan with the basil, salt, and butter. Heat until it starts to bubble. Slowly stir in cornstarch to thicken.

In a frying pan, brown the beef and onions; drain if necessary. Stir in cumin. Spoon the beef mixture into the bottom of a greased 9 x 13-inch pan. Sprinkle olives and raisins over beef mixture. Spread corn mixture evenly over top. Sprinkle sugar over corn layer. Bake for 40–50 minutes, or until golden brown.

NOTE: This traditional Chilean dish, called *pastel de choclo,* is often served with more sugar on the side.

Quick Tamale Pie

Makes 4–6 servings.

1 pound ground beef
1 (14.75-ounce) can
    cream-style corn
1 envelope taco
    seasoning
1 (3.8-ounce) can sliced
    olives, drained
1 (6.5-ounce) package
    corn bread mix

Preheat oven to 400 degrees.

In a large frying pan, brown the ground beef until no longer pink. Stir in the corn and taco seasoning. Spoon the mixture into a greased deep-dish pie pan. Sprinkle the olives over the meat. Prepare the corn bread batter according to package directions. Spread batter evenly over top. Bake for 15–17 minutes, or until golden brown.

Saucy Baked Meatballs

Makes 8 servings.

1 pound ground beef
1/2 pound ground sausage
3/4 cup applesauce
1 cup fine dry
    breadcrumbs
1 teaspoon salt
1/4 teaspoon pepper
1 (10.75-ounce) can
    tomato soup,
    condensed
1/4 cup water

Preheat oven to 375 degrees.

In a large bowl, combine the ground beef, sausage, applesauce, breadcrumbs, salt, and pepper. Shape into 24 meatballs. Place meatballs in a 2-quart baking dish.

In a small bowl, blend the tomato soup and water. Pour over meatballs, cover, and bake for 1 hour, or until meatballs are no longer pink in the center.

Meatball Casserole

1 (10.75-ounce) can
    cream of chicken
    soup, condensed
1 cup sour cream
1 cup grated cheddar
    cheese
1 large onion, chopped
1 teaspoon salt
1 teaspoon black pepper
1 (30-ounce) bag frozen
    shredded hash
    browns, thawed
20 precooked frozen
    meatballs

Preheat oven to 350 degrees.

In a bowl, stir together the soup, sour cream, cheese, onion, salt, and pepper. With a paper towel, pat the hash browns dry and then stir into the soup mixture. Spread hash brown mixture into a greased 9 x 13-inch pan. Slightly press meatballs into mixture in even rows. Cover with aluminum foil and bake for 35 minutes. Uncover and bake for 10–15 minutes more, or until hash browns are done.

Corn Flake Meatballs

Makes 4–6 servings.

1 pound ground beef
1 egg, beaten
1/4 cup applesauce
1/2 cup crushed corn
    flakes
1 small onion, chopped
1/2 teaspoon salt
1/4 teaspoon pepper
1/4 teaspoon garlic salt
1 (10.75-ounce) can
    cream of mushroom
    soup, condensed
1 cup milk

Preheat oven to 350 degrees.

In a large bowl, combine all of the ingredients except the mushroom soup and milk. Shape into 18 meatballs. Place the meatballs in a greased 9 x 13-inch pan. In a 1-quart bowl, whisk together cream of mushroom soup and milk until smooth. Pour soup mixture over top and bake uncovered for 45–50 minutes.

Porcupine Meatballs

Makes 4–6 servings.

1 (10.75-ounce) can
  condensed tomato
  soup, divided
1 pound ground beef
1 cup uncooked instant
  rice
1 egg, beaten
1/4 medium onion,
  chopped
1 teaspoon salt
1/2 teaspoon pepper
3/4 cup water
1 teaspoon yellow
  mustard
2–3 cloves garlic,
  minced

Preheat oven to 350 degrees.

In a large bowl, combine 1/4 cup soup, ground beef, rice, egg, onion, salt, and pepper. Shape into 18 meatballs and place them in a 9 x 13-inch pan prepared with nonstick cooking spray.

In a separate bowl, mix the remaining soup, water, mustard, and garlic. Pour mixture over meatballs. Bake uncovered for 45–50 minutes.

Beef-Stuffed Eggplant

Makes 4 servings.

2 medium eggplants, halved
1 pound ground beef
1 (16-ounce) can stewed tomatoes, with liquid
1 (8-ounce) can tomato sauce
1 teaspoon salt
$1/4$ teaspoon oregano
$1/4$ teaspoon garlic salt
$1/2$ cup grated Parmesan cheese

Preheat oven to 350 degrees.

Cut ends from eggplants. Carefully cut each eggplant lengthwise down the center, and scoop out flesh, leaving a $1/4$-inch shell and making sure not to break. Place eggplant shells in a baking pan and set aside. Chop eggplant centers and add to a large frying pan with the ground beef. Brown the ground beef until no longer pink. Add the tomatoes, tomato sauce, salt, oregano, and garlic salt. Simmer over low heat for 15–20 minutes, stirring occasionally. Remove from heat and stir in the cheese. Spoon the mixture into the eggplant shells. Bake in a greased 9 x 13-inch pan for 25 minutes, or until eggplant shell is tender.

Stuffed Tomatoes Topped with Breadcrumbs

Makes 6 *servings.*

6 medium tomatoes
1 pound ground beef
$1/4$ cup minced onion
1 cup milk
$1/4$ cup flour
1 teaspoon salt
$1/4$ teaspoon pepper
1 teaspoon curry powder
$1/2$ cup buttered breadcrumbs

Preheat oven to 350 degrees.

Cut a very thin slice from the top of tomatoes and carefully spoon out centers. Turn tomato "cups" upside down to drain; set aside.

In a frying pan, brown the ground beef with onion until meat is no longer pink and onion is transparent.

In a small bowl, combine the milk, flour, salt, pepper, and curry. Pour mixture into meat and bring to a boil over medium-low heat and boil 1 minute. Spoon meat mixture into the tomato cups. Place tomato cups in a 9 x 13-inch baking pan and sprinkle tops with the breadcrumbs. Bake for 17–20 minutes, or until golden brown.

Grandma's Stuffed Bell Peppers

Makes 6 servings.

6 green bell peppers
1 pound ground beef
1 medium onion,
**   chopped**
1 (14.5-ounce) can
**   Italian-style diced**
**   tomatoes, with liquid**
³/₄ cup uncooked instant
**   white rice**
1¹/₄ cups water, divided
Salt and pepper, to taste
¹/₃ cup seasoned
**   breadcrumbs**

Preheat oven to 350 degrees.

Bring a large pot of salted water to a boil. Cut the tops off the bell peppers. Remove seeds. Parboil the peppers in boiling water for 5 minutes. Carefully remove peppers and drain any excess water.

In a frying pan, brown the ground beef and onion until meat is no longer pink; drain if necessary. Stir in the tomatoes, rice, and ³/₄ cup water. Cover and simmer over medium heat for 5 minutes, or until rice is tender; remove from heat. Season with salt and pepper. Stuff each pepper with beef and rice mixture. Place stuffed peppers open side up in a 9 x 13-inch baking dish. Sprinkle tops with breadcrumbs. Pour ¹/₂ cup water in bottom of baking dish. Cover with aluminum foil and bake for 30 minutes, or until heated through.

Aunt Leara's Zucchini Boats

Makes 4–6 *servings.*

3 medium zucchini,
   peeled
1 pound ground beef
1 medium onion,
   chopped
1 (8-ounce) can tomato
   sauce
1½ teaspoons Italian
   seasoning salt
1½ cups grated
   mozzarella cheese

Preheat oven to 350 degrees.

Cut the zucchini in half lengthwise and then scoop out seeds to form a boat. Bring a large pot of salted water to a boil. Boil zucchini for 5 minutes. Remove zucchini and drain. Place in bottom of a lightly greased 9 x 13-inch pan.

In a frying pan, brown the ground beef and onion until meat is no longer pink. Stir in the tomato sauce and Italian seasoning. Fill the zucchini with the meat mixture. Sprinkle cheese evenly over top. Bake for 20 minutes, or until heated through and cheese melts.

Baked Italian Delight

Makes 6–8 servings.

1 pound ground beef
1 (26-ounce) jar chunky
   spaghetti sauce
1 cup cottage cheese
1/4 cup grated Parmesan
   cheese
1 egg, slightly beaten
2 (8-count each) tubes
   crescent rolls
1 cup grated mozzarella
   cheese

Preheat oven to 375 degrees.

In a large frying pan, brown the ground beef until no longer pink; drain if necessary. Stir in the spaghetti sauce and simmer for 5 minutes over low heat.

In a bowl, combine the cottage cheese, Parmesan cheese, and egg. Lay 1 tube crescent roll dough along the bottom of a 9 x 13-inch pan. Press together the perforations to form a crust. Layer half the meat mixture, cottage cheese mixture, then remaining meat mixture. Sprinkle mozzarella cheese over top. Lay the remaining dough over top, covering as much as possible. Bake for 25 minutes, or until golden brown.

Pork Main Dishes

Broccoli and Ham Pot Pie

Makes 4–6 servings.

Preheat oven to 425 degrees.

1 (10-ounce) package frozen chopped broccoli, thawed
1 (15-ounce) can whole kernel corn, drained
1 (10.75-ounce) can cream of mushroom soup, condensed
2 cups chopped fully cooked ham
1 1/2 cups grated cheddar cheese
3/4 cup sour cream
1/2 teaspoon black pepper
1 refrigerated pie crust

Spread the broccoli into the bottom of a lightly greased and microwaveable 10-inch deep-dish pie pan or a 1 1/2-quart round dish; set aside.

In a bowl, mix together the corn, soup, ham, cheese, sour cream, and pepper. Spoon the mixture over the broccoli. Cover with a paper towel and microwave on high heat for 3–4 1/2 minutes, or until hot. Place the unfolded pie crust over ham mixture and tuck the edges inside the pan. Cut four 1-inch slits in the crust to allow steam to escape during baking. Place the pan on top of a baking sheet. Bake for 15 minutes, or until the crust turns golden brown.

Country-Style Broccoli, Ham, and Cheese

Makes 4–6 *servings.*

1 (10-ounce) package
    frozen broccoli
1 cup diced fully cooked
    ham
1 (10.75-ounce) can
    cheddar cheese soup,
    condensed
1/2 cup sour cream
2 cups breadcrumbs
1 tablespoon butter or
    margarine, melted

Preheat oven to 350 degrees.

Cook the broccoli according to package directions; drain and set aside.

In a large bowl, combine all of the ingredients except the breadcrumbs and butter. Transfer the mixture into a greased 9 x 13-inch pan. Combine the breadcrumbs and butter and then sprinkle over top. Bake for 30–35 minutes.

Ham and Swiss Pork Chops

Makes 4–6 *servings.*

6 pork chops
1 tablespoon butter or
    margarine
12 fresh bay leaves
6 slices ham
2 tablespoons chopped
    fresh sage
1 cup grated Swiss
    cheese

Preheat oven to 375 degrees.

In a frying pan, brown the pork chops in butter for 2–3 minutes on each side. Set on a plate lined with paper towels to drain. In a greased 9 x 13-inch pan, layer the pork chops, bay leaves, ham, sage, and cheese. Cover with aluminum foil and bake for 25 minutes.

Broccoli, Cheddar, and Ham Strata

Makes 6–8 *servings.*

1 tablespoon olive oil
1 medium onion, diced
1 pound frozen chopped
  broccoli, thawed
1 (14-ounce) loaf Italian
  bread, cut into cubes
1/2 pound fully cooked
  ham, chopped
6 large eggs
1 1/2 cups milk
2 tablespoons chopped
  chives
1 tablespoon Dijon
  mustard
1/2 teaspoon salt
1/4 teaspoon black
  pepper
1 1/2 cups grated cheddar
  cheese

Preheat oven to 375 degrees.

Prepare a 9 x 13-inch baking dish with nonstick spray; set aside. Heat the oil in a large nonstick skillet over medium heat. Add the onion and saute for 5 minutes. Add the broccoli and cook another 3 minutes. Place the bread cubes in a large bowl. Stir in the broccoli mixture and the ham.

In a medium bowl, whisk together the eggs, milk, chives, mustard, salt, and pepper. Pour the mixture over the bread, stirring to combine. Transfer to the prepared baking dish and top evenly with the cheese. Bake for 40–45 minutes. Serve warm.

NOTE: French bread can be substituted for the Italian bread if you prefer.

Simple Pork and Rice Dinner

Makes 4–6 *servings.*

1 tablespoon vegetable oil
1 pound lean pork, cut into cubes
$1/2$ cup chopped onion
1 cup chopped celery
$1^1/2$–2 cups long-grain white rice
1 (10.75-ounce) can cream of chicken soup, condensed
1 cup water
3 tablespoons soy sauce

Preheat oven to 350 degrees.

Prepare a 9 x 13-inch baking dish with nonstick cooking spray and set aside. Heat the oil over medium heat; brown the pork and then add the onion and celery. Continue cooking until onion is golden, about 2–3 minutes. Add all of the remaining ingredients and stir to combine. Pour into the prepared baking dish. Cover with aluminum foil and bake for 1 hour.

Sweet and Sour Pork Casserole

Makes 6–8 *servings.*

1 pound lean pork, cubed
$^3/_4$ cup diced onion
1 tablespoon butter
1 (8-ounce) can
    pineapple tidbits
$^1/_2$ cup diced green bell
    pepper
$^1/_2$ cup diced red bell
    pepper
2 tablespoons brown
    sugar
1 tablespoon soy sauce
2 teaspoons
    Worcestershire sauce
2 tablespoons ketchup
2 tablespoons white
    vinegar
1 tablespoon cornstarch
$^1/_2$ teaspoon salt
$1^1/_2$ cups long-grain
    white rice
3 cups water

Preheat oven to 300 degrees.

Cook the pork for 2–3 minutes in a large skillet, stirring constantly. Place the meat in a 9 x 13-inch baking dish lightly sprayed with nonstick spray; set aside. Cook the onion in the same pan that was used for the pork, adding the butter. Cook the onion for 3 minutes. Add the pineapple with liquid to the pan with the onions; add the bell peppers. Stir in the sugar, soy sauce, Worcestershire, and ketchup.

In a small bowl, mix together the vinegar, cornstarch, and salt. Add the mixture to saucepan and cook for 1 minute. Add thickened mixture to the pork in the baking dish. Add rice and water and stir to combine. Cover with aluminum foil and cook for 1 to $1^1/_2$ hours, or until rice is done.

Pork Chops with Orange Rice

Makes 6 servings.

6 pork chops
Salt and pepper, to taste
1⅓ cups uncooked
   white rice
1 cup orange juice
1 (10.5-ounce) can
   chicken and rice
   soup, condensed

Preheat oven to 350 degrees.

In a frying pan, brown the pork chops for 2 minutes on each side and season with salt and pepper; set aside.

In a greased 9 x 13-inch pan, combine the rice and orange juice. Place the pork chops over the rice and pour the soup over top. Cover with aluminum foil and bake for 45 minutes. Uncover and cook for 10 minutes more or until done.

Pork Chop, Mushroom, and Rice Casserole

Makes 4 servings.

1¼ cups uncooked long
   grain rice
4 pork chops
1½ tablespoons olive oil
1 container (5-6 ounces)
   sliced mushrooms
3 cups water, divided
1 envelope dry onion
   soup mix
1 (10.75-ounce) can
   cream of mushroom
   soup, condensed

Preheat oven to 350 degrees.

Sprinkle the uncooked rice evenly over the bottom of a 9 x 9-inch pan prepared with nonstick cooking spray.

In a large skillet, brown the pork chops in hot olive oil over medium-high heat for 1½ minutes on each side. Place the pork chops over the rice. Sprinkle the mushrooms over top. In the skillet where the pork chops were cooked, stir 2½ cups water and dry onion soup mix into hot drippings. Evenly pour the mixture over the pork chops.

In a separate bowl, combine the soup and ½ cup water until smooth. Spoon the soup mixture evenly over the pork chops. Cover the pan with aluminum foil and bake for 45 minutes. Uncover and bake 15 minutes more or until the internal temperature of the pork reaches 160 degrees.

Mexican Pork Chops and Rice

Makes 4 servings.

4 boneless pork chops
2 tablespoons olive oil
1 medium onion,
chopped
1 teaspoon minced garlic
1 (15-ounce) can black
beans, rinsed and
drained
1 (15-ounce) can whole
kernel corn, drained
1 (10.75-ounce) can
tomato soup,
condensed
1¼ cups water
1 cup uncooked instant
rice
1½ teaspoons chili
powder
1½ teaspoons dried
cilantro
½ teaspoon cumin
½ teaspoon salt
¼ teaspoon pepper

Preheat oven to 350 degrees.

In a large skillet, brown the pork chops in the oil for 3 minutes on each side. Remove pork chops. Add the onion and garlic to the drippings in pan and saute until tender. Add all of the remaining ingredients and stir. Pour the mixture into a 9 x 9-inch pan prepared with nonstick cooking spray. Place the pork chops over top. Cover with aluminum foil and bake for 35–40 minutes.

Ham and Cheese Enchiladas

Makes 8–10 *servings.*

2 cups cubed fully cooked ham

⅓ cup chopped green onions

⅓ cup chopped green bell pepper

10 (8-inch) flour tortillas

2 cups grated cheddar cheese, divided

6 eggs

2 cups half-and-half

1 tablespoon flour

¼ teaspoon salt

¼ teaspoon pepper

In a bowl, combine the ham, onions, and bell pepper. Place a heaping ¼ cup of the mixture down the center of each tortilla. Sprinkle 2 tablespoons cheese over filling in each tortilla. Roll the filled tortillas and place seam side down in a 9 x 13-inch pan prepared with nonstick cooking spray.

In a 2-quart bowl, whisk the eggs until smooth. Mix in the half-and-half, flour, salt, and pepper. Pour the mixture evenly over the tortillas. Cover with aluminum foil and refrigerate for 6 hours or overnight. Remove casserole from the refrigerator for 30 minutes before baking.

Preheat oven to 350 degrees. Bake covered with aluminum foil for 30 minutes. Uncover and sprinkle enchiladas with remaining cheese. Bake uncovered for 15–20 minutes more, or until cheese is melted and center is set. Cool for 5 minutes before serving.

Bell Pepper Stuffing Casserole

Makes 4–6 *servings.*

1 pound ground spicy
  pork sausage
1/2 cup chopped onion
1 green bell pepper,
  diced
1 teaspoon minced garlic
1/2 teaspoon ground
  cumin
1 (28-ounce) can diced
  tomatoes, with liquid
1 (14.5-ounce) can
  chicken broth
1 cup uncooked long-
  grain rice
1/4 teaspoon salt
1/2 teaspoon pepper
1/4 teaspoon cayenne
  pepper

Preheat oven to 350 degrees.

In a large skillet, brown and crumble the sausage until no longer pink; drain if necessary. Add the onion, bell pepper, garlic, and cumin and saute for 2 minutes. Add the tomatoes, chicken broth, uncooked rice, salt, pepper, and cayenne pepper. Pour the mixture into a 9 x 13-inch pan prepared with nonstick cooking spray. Cover with aluminum foil and bake for 45 minutes. Uncover and bake 15 minutes more, or until rice is tender and most of the liquid is absorbed.

NOTE: For a really spicy version, increase the amount of cayenne pepper to 1 teaspoon and stir in 1 (4-ounce) can green chiles before baking.

Easiest Sausage and Rice Casserole

Makes 6–8 servings.

1 pound pork sausage,
   browned and drained
1/2 cup chopped celery
1/2 cup chopped onion
1/2 cup chopped green
   bell pepper
2 (10.75-ounce) cans
   cream of chicken
   soup, condensed
2 cans water
1 cup long-grain white
   rice

Preheat oven to 325 degrees.

Prepare a 9 x 13-inch baking dish with nonstick spray and set aside.

In a large bowl, combine all of the ingredients. Pour into the prepared baking dish and bake for 1 1/2 hours.

Sausage Jambalaya

Makes 6–8 *servings.*

1/2 cup butter or margarine
1 large onion, chopped
1 large green bell pepper, chopped
1/2 cup diced celery
1 tablespoon minced garlic
1 pound fully cooked smoked sausage links, cut into 1-inch slices
3 cups chicken broth
2 cups uncooked white rice
1 cup chopped tomatoes
1/2 cup chopped green onion
1 1/2 tablespoons parsley
1 tablespoon Worcestershire sauce
1 tablespoon Tabasco sauce

Preheat oven to 375 degrees.

In a frying pan, melt the butter and saute the onion, bell pepper, celery, and garlic until tender. In a large bowl, combine the sausage, broth, rice, tomatoes, green onion, parsley, Worcestershire sauce, and Tabasco sauce. Stir the sauteed vegetables into the sausage mixture. Spread the mixture into a greased 9 x 13-inch pan. Cover with aluminum foil and bake for 20 minutes. Stir, cover, and bake 20 minutes more. Stir, cover, and bake a final 5–10 minutes, or until rice is done.

Sausage and Green Bean Casserole

Makes 8–10 *servings.*

1 pound Italian ground sausage
1 (8-ounce) container fresh sliced mushrooms
1 teaspoon minced garlic
2 (10.75-ounce) cans cream of mushroom soup, condensed
1 cup milk
1/4 teaspoon pepper
1 (28-ounce) bags frozen cut green beans, thawed
1 (2.8-ounce) can french-fried onions

Preheat oven to 350 degrees.

In a large skillet, brown the sausage until it is crumbly and no longer pink; drain if necessary. Stir in the mushrooms and garlic; set aside.

In a large bowl, whisk together the soup, milk, and pepper until smooth. Stir the sausage mixture into soup. Fold the green beans into the mixture until evenly coated. Spread half the bean mixture in a 9 x 13-inch pan that has been prepared with nonstick cooking spray. Sprinkle half the onions evenly over top. Spread the remaining bean mixture over the onions. Bake for 30 minutes. Top with the remaining onions and bake for 5–10 minutes more.

Tater Tot Sausage Casserole

Makes 8–10 *servings.*

2 pounds frozen tater tots
1 pound Italian ground sausage
1 cup onion, chopped
1 teaspoon minced garlic
2 cups grated cheddar cheese
2 cups milk
4 eggs
1/4 teaspoon pepper

Preheat oven to 450 degrees.

Place the tater tots on a sheet pan and bake for 10 minutes. (They won't be thoroughly cooked until baked in the casserole.) Reduce oven temperature to 350 degrees.

In a frying pan, brown the sausage, onion, and garlic until crumbly and cooked through; drain if necessary. Spread sausage mixture evenly over the bottom of 9 x 13-inch pan prepared with nonstick cooking spray. Layer the cheese over top.

In a bowl, whisk together the milk, eggs, and pepper. Pour evenly over the cheese. Top casserole with the partially baked tater tots. Bake uncovered at 350 degrees for 45 minutes. Cool for 5 minutes before serving.

Meaty Italian Penne Casserole

Makes 4–5 *servings.*

8 ounces penne pasta
1 pound Italian ground sausage
1 teaspoon minced garlic
1 (26-ounce) jar spaghetti sauce, any variety
1 cup mini pepperoni slices
1 (8-ounce) package grated mozzarella cheese, divided

Preheat oven to 350 degrees.

Cook the pasta according to package directions until al dente; drain and set aside.

In a large skillet, brown the sausage until it is crumbly and no longer pink; drain if necessary. Spoon the sausage into a large bowl. Stir in the garlic, spaghetti sauce, and pepperoni. Fold in the drained pasta and half the cheese. Spoon the mixture into a 9 x 13-inch pan prepared with nonstick cooking spray. Sprinkle the remaining cheese over top. Bake for 20–25 minutes, or until bubbly.

Pepperoni and Sausage Biscuit Bake

Makes 4–6 *servings.*

1 pound ground sausage
1 medium onion,
    chopped
1 (3.5-ounce) package
    sliced pepperoni
1 (14-ounce) jar pizza
    sauce
1¼ cups grated
    mozzarella cheese
1 cup biscuit mix
1 cup milk
2 eggs, lightly beaten

Preheat oven to 400 degrees.

In a frying pan, brown the sausage and onion together until sausage is done. Drain any excess grease and then stir in the pepperoni. Spread the mixture into a greased 8 x 8-inch pan. Pour the sauce evenly over meat and sprinkle the cheese over top.

In a separate bowl, mix together the biscuit mix, milk, and eggs. Pour the batter evenly over top. Bake uncovered for 25 minutes, or until golden brown.

Chili Corn Dog Casserole

Makes 6–8 servings.

2 (15-ounce) cans chili
1 (16-ounce) package hot
   dogs, thinly sliced
1 (8.5-ounce) package
   corn bread mix

Preheat oven to 400 degrees.

Spread the chili into a 9 x 13-inch pan prepared with nonstick cooking spray. Arrange the hotdog slices evenly over top. Prepare the corn bread mix according to package directions. Pour the batter evenly over the hot dogs and spread to cover completely. Bake for 25 minutes, or until the corn bread is golden and set in the center.

Baked Beans 'n' Dogs

Makes 6–8 servings.

3 (15-ounce) cans pork
   and beans
1 package (16-ounce)
   hot dogs, sliced
1/2 cup brown sugar
1/4 cup ketchup
1/4 cup dried minced
   onion
2 teaspoons mustard

Preheat oven to 350 degrees.

Mix all ingredients together in a 2- to 3-quart baking dish. Bake uncovered for 45 minutes, or until bubbly.

Easy Ham and Hash Brown Dinner

Makes 8–10 *servings.*

2 (10.75-ounce) cans cream of potato soup, condensed*

1½ cups grated cheddar cheese

1½ cups fully cooked cubed ham

1 (26–32-ounce) bag frozen shredded hash browns, thawed

1 cup french-fried onions

Preheat oven to 350 degrees.

In a large bowl, combine the soup, cheese, ham, and hash browns together. Press into a greased 9 x 13-inch pan. Bake uncovered for 55–65 minutes, or until golden brown and bubbly around the edges. During the last 5–10 minutes of cooking time, sprinkle the french–fried onions over top.

*Cream of mushroom or chicken soups can be substituted.

Creamy Potato Bake with Ham and Broccoli

Makes 8 servings.

1 (10.75-ounce) can cream of broccoli soup, condensed
3/4 cup milk
1/2 teaspoon salt
1/4 teaspoon pepper
1 1/2 cups cubed fully cooked ham
2 cups frozen chopped broccoli
1 (24-ounce) bag frozen shredded hash browns
1 cup crushed cornflakes

Preheat oven to 350 degrees.

In a large bowl, stir together the soup, milk, salt, pepper, ham, and broccoli. Fold in the hash browns. Spread the mixture evenly over the bottom of a lightly greased 9 x 13-inch pan. Sprinkle the cornflakes over top. Cover with aluminum foil and bake for 45–55 minutes, or until hot in the center and bubbly around the edges. For a crispier top, remove aluminum foil during the last 10–15 minutes of baking.

Bacon and Hash Brown Heaven

Makes 6–8 *servings.*

4 cups frozen shredded
   hash browns, thawed
1 pound bacon, cooked
   and crumbled
1½ cups cubed fully
   cooked ham
⅔ cup milk
½ cup chopped onion
½ teaspoon salt
¼ teaspoon black pepper
⅛ teaspoon garlic
   powder (optional)
2 tablespoons butter or
   margarine, melted

Preheat oven to 350 degrees.

Combine all of the ingredients in a large bowl. Transfer to a greased 8 x 8-inch pan. Bake for 45 minutes.

NOTE: Make it cheesy by sprinkling 1 cup grated cheddar cheese over casserole immediately after baking.

Chicken and Turkey Dishes

Grandma's Chicken Pot Pie

Makes 5–7 servings.

Preheat oven to 400 degrees.

2 cups frozen Normandy or California-style vegetables

1½ cups cubed cooked chicken

2 (10.75-ounce) cans cream of chicken soup, condensed

¾ cup milk

½ teaspoon thyme or rosemary

1½ teaspoons black pepper

1 (10-ounce) tube refrigerated flaky biscuits

Cook and cut vegetables into bite-size pieces.

In a greased 3-quart baking dish, combine all of the ingredients except the biscuits. Bake uncovered for 15 minutes; remove from oven and stir. Quickly cut biscuits in half. Place biscuit halves, cut side down, over hot chicken and vegetable mixture. Bake for 15–20 minutes more, or until biscuits are golden brown and done in the center.

Easy Chicken Pot Pie

Makes 8 *servings.*

1 (12.5-ounce) can
   chicken breast
   chunks, drained
1 cup milk
2 (10.75-ounce) cans
   cream of chicken
   soup, condensed
1 (16-ounce) bag frozen
   mixed vegetables
1/2 teaspoon salt
2 (14.5-ounce) cans
   diced new potatoes,
   drained
2 (8-ounce) tubes
   crescent rolls

Preheat oven to 400 degrees.

In a large frying pan, combine the chicken, milk, and soup. Cook over medium-low heat, stirring constantly. When it starts bubbling, add the mixed vegetables, salt, and potatoes. Simmer on low heat for 5–7 minutes. Roll out 1 can of crescent roll dough and place in bottom of a 9 x 13-inch pan. Pour filling over crust. Separate second can of crescent rolls. Place the triangles over top, covering as much as possible. Bake for 15 minutes, or until crescents are golden brown.

Broccoli Chicken Casserole

Makes 4–6 servings.

Preheat oven to 350 degrees.

In a large bowl, mix together all of the ingredients. Spread the mixture into a greased 9 x 13-inch pan. Bake for 35–40 minutes, or until bubbly.

2 cups chopped cooked chicken

1 (10.75-ounce) can cream of mushroom soup, condensed

1/4 cup milk

3/4 cup grated Monterey Jack cheese

1 (10-ounce) bag frozen broccoli, thawed

1/2 cup sliced green onion

1/2 teaspoon black pepper

Cheesy Chicken

4–6 boneless, skinless
  chicken breasts
1 (16-ounce) container
  sour cream
1 (10.75-ounce) can
  cream of celery soup,
  condensed
1 (10.75-ounce) can
  cream of chicken
  soup, condensed
1¼ cups water
2 cups uncooked white
  rice
1 cup grated cheddar
  cheese

Preheat oven to 325 degrees.

Place the chicken in a greased 9 x 13-inch pan.

In a bowl, combine sour cream, soups, water, and uncooked rice. Pour the mixture over the chicken. Cover with aluminum foil and bake for 1 hour. Sprinkle with cheese immediately before serving.

Ritzy Chicken

Makes 4 servings.

4 boneless, skinless chicken breasts
1 (10.75-ounce) can cream of chicken soup, condensed
1 (10.75-ounce) can broccoli cheese soup, condensed
1 1/3 cups milk
1 1/2 cups sour cream
2 cups cooked white rice
25–35 butter-flavored crackers, crumbled

Preheat oven to 375 degrees.

Place the chicken in a greased 9 x 13-inch pan.

In a bowl, combine all of the remaining ingredients except the crackers. Pour the mixture over the chicken. Bake for 45 minutes, or until the chicken is done. During the last 5–10 minutes of baking, sprinkle cracker crumbs over top.

Poppy Seed Stuffing Chicken

Makes 6–8 *servings.*

4–5 chicken breasts, cooked and chopped
Olive oil
Salt and pepper, to taste
2 (10.75-ounce) cans cream of chicken soup
1 cup sour cream
2 tablespoons poppy seeds
2 cups seasoned corn bread stuffing mix (little cubes, not instant)
1 stick butter, cut into pieces

Preheat oven to 350 degrees.

Broil the chicken with a little olive oil, salt, and pepper until done; cool slightly and chop. Place the chicken in a greased 9 x 13-inch baking dish.

In a medium bowl, combine the soup, sour cream, and poppy seeds. Pour over the chicken and stir to blend. Sprinkle the stuffing mix over the top of chicken mixture. Place butter pieces evenly over the stuffing. Bake for about 30–40 minutes, or until bubbly.

Corn Bread Chicken-Vegetable Casserole

Makes 6–8 *servings.*

1 (2.25-pound) cooked lemon pepper rotisserie chicken

1 (16-ounce) bag frozen mixed vegetables, thawed and drained

1 (10.75-ounce) can cream of chicken soup, condensed

1 (10.75-ounce) can cream of onion soup, condensed

$1/2$ teaspoon black pepper

1 (8.5-ounce) box corn muffin mix, mixed according to directions

Preheat oven to 350 degrees. Shred the cooked chicken meat.

In a bowl, combine the chicken, vegetables, soups, and pepper. Spread the mixture into a greased 9 x 13-inch pan prepared with nonstick cooking spray. Pour the corn bread batter evenly over the chicken layer. Bake for 30–35 minutes, or until golden brown and bubbly.

Swiss Chicken

4–6 boneless, skinless chicken breasts

4–6 slices Swiss cheese

1 (10.75-ounce) can cream of mushroom or chicken soup, condensed

¼ cup milk

1 (6-ounce) box seasoned stuffing mix

¼ cup butter or margarine, melted

Preheat oven to 350 degrees.

Lay chicken in the bottom of a greased 9 x 13-inch pan. Place the cheese slices over chicken.

In a bowl, mix together the soup and milk. Pour the mixture over the chicken. Sprinkle the dry stuffing mix over top and drizzle with the butter. Cover with aluminum foil and bake for 55–65 minutes, or until chicken is done.

Baked Chicken Stuffing

Makes 8 servings.

Preheat oven to 350 degrees.

2 (10.75-ounce) cans cream of celery or cream of onion soup, condensed

1 1/2 cups water

1 (6-ounce) box chicken-flavored stuffing mix

2 cups grated carrots

2 (14.5-ounce) cans cut green beans, drained

2 1/2 cups diced cooked chicken

In a large bowl, whisk together the soup and water. Fold the dry stuffing mix into soup. Gently stir in the carrots, green beans, and chicken until combined. Spoon the mixture into a 9 x 13-inch pan prepared with nonstick cooking spray. Bake uncovered for 35–40 minutes, until golden brown.

Wild Rice and Garlic-Basil Chicken

Makes 4 servings.

Preheat oven to 375 degrees.

1 (6.2-ounce) box long grain and wild rice, with seasoning packet

1 1/2 cups water

4 boneless, skinless chicken breasts

1/2 teaspoon dried basil

1/2 teaspoon garlic powder

In a bowl, combine the rice, seasoning packet, and water. Pour the mixture into a greased 9 x 13-inch pan. Place the chicken over the rice mixture and sprinkle with the basil and garlic powder. Cover with aluminum foil and bake for 1 hour.

Creamy Chicken and Rice

Makes 4–6 servings.

2 cups uncooked white
   rice
2 (10.75-ounce) cans
   cream of chicken
   soup, condensed
2 cups water
1 envelope onion soup
   mix, divided
4–6 boneless, skinless
   chicken breasts

Preheat oven to 375 degrees.

In a bowl, combine the rice, chicken soup, water, and half the onion soup mix. Spread mixture into a greased 9 x 13-inch pan. Lay the chicken over top. Sprinkle the remaining onion soup mix over the chicken. Cover with aluminum foil and bake for 2 hours.

NOTE: This casserole can also be baked at 300 degrees for 3 hours.

Curry Chicken and Wild Rice

Makes 6–8 *servings*

1 (6-ounce) box long grain and wild rice, cooked according to directions

4 cups cooked diced chicken

2 (10.75-ounce) cans cream of chicken soup

1 cup sour cream

2 teaspoons curry powder, or to taste

1 (6-ounce) package corn bread stuffing mix

$1/2$ cup unsalted butter, cut into small pieces

Preheat oven to 350 degrees.

Layer the rice in the bottom of a greased 2-quart baking dish. Layer the chicken on top of rice.

In a bowl, mix together the soup, sour cream, and curry powder and pour evenly over the chicken. Sprinkle the stuffing mix over top and dot with small pieces of butter. Bake for 30 minutes, or until bubbly.

Green Bean Chicken Casserole

Makes 4 servings.

1 tablespoon olive oil

4 boneless, skinless chicken breasts

3–4 (14.5-ounce) cans French-cut green beans, drained

1 (10.75-ounce) can cream of mushroom or chicken soup, condensed

3/4 cup mayonnaise

1 teaspoon garlic powder

1/3 cup grated Parmesan cheese

Preheat oven to 350 degrees.

In a large frying pan, heat the oil. Lightly brown the chicken for 3 minutes on each side. Meanwhile, spread the green beans evenly in the bottom of a greased 9 x 13-inch pan. Lay the chicken over the beans.

In a bowl, combine the soup, mayonnaise, and garlic powder. Spread the mixture evenly over the chicken and beans. Sprinkle the Parmesan over top. Bake uncovered for 35–40 minutes, or until chicken is done.

Home-Style Chicken Casserole

Makes 6 servings.

4 cups frozen shredded hash browns, thawed

1 (6-ounce) can french-fried onions, divided

6 slices processed American cheese

2 boneless, skinless chicken breasts, cubed

1 (10.75-ounce) can cream of chicken soup, condensed

3/4 cup milk

1 (12-ounce) can whole kernel corn, drained

Preheat oven to 375 degrees.

In a bowl, stir together the hash browns and half the onions. Spread the mixture into a greased 9 x 13-inch pan. Lay the cheese slices evenly over the hash browns. Place the chicken cubes evenly over top.

In a bowl, stir together the soup and milk. Pour the mixture over the chicken. Bake uncovered for 30 minutes. Spoon the corn over top and then stir in the pan. Bake uncovered for 15 minutes more. Sprinkle the remaining onions over top. Bake for 5 minutes more. Let cool 5–7 minutes before serving.

Honey Mustard Chicken and Potato Casserole

Makes 8 servings.

2 (10.75-ounce) cans cream of chicken soup, condensed
$3/4$ cup mayonnaise
$1/2$ cup milk
$1/4$ cup honey
2 tablespoons mustard
2–3 cups cooked cubed chicken*
1 (30-ounce) bag frozen shredded hash browns

Preheat oven to 350 degrees.

In a large bowl, mix together the soup, mayonnaise, milk, honey, and mustard until smooth. Stir in the chicken and hash browns. Spread the mixture into a greased 9 x 13-inch pan. Cover with aluminum foil and bake for 40–50 minutes. Uncover and bake for 10–15 minutes more, or until golden brown and bubbly around the edges.

*Canned chicken breast can be substituted.

Teriyaki Chicken

Makes 4 servings.

2 boneless, skinless chicken breasts, cubed

1 (15-ounce) can chicken broth

2 tablespoons brown sugar

2 tablespoons soy sauce

$1/2$ teaspoon ground ginger

$1/2$ teaspoon Worcestershire sauce

1 cup uncooked white rice

1 (8-ounce) can pineapple chunks, drained

Preheat oven to 350 degrees.

Combine all of the ingredients in a large bowl. Transfer the mixture into a greased 9 x 13-inch pan. Cover with aluminum foil and bake for 1 hour, or until rice is done.

Cashew Chicken

Makes 2–4 servings.

1 (6.2-ounce) box fried
  rice, with seasoning
  packet
2 cups water
2 boneless, skinless
  chicken breasts,
  cooked and cubed
½ cup sliced celery
1 (4-ounce) can sliced
  water chestnuts,
  drained
⅔ cup cashews

Preheat oven to 350 degrees.

In a bowl, combine the rice, sea-soning packet, and water. Layer the chicken, rice mixture, celery, and water chestnuts in a greased 9 x 9-inch pan. Cover with aluminum foil and bake for 30–40 minutes, or until rice is done. Sprinkle with the cashews and serve.

Tortilla Chip Enchiladas

Makes 6–8 servings.

2 cups chopped cooked
  chicken
2 (10.75-ounce) cans
  cream of chicken
  soup, condensed
1 cup sour cream
¼ cup chopped onion
1 (12-ounce) bag tortilla
  chips, crushed in bag
1 cup grated Monterey
  Jack cheese
1½ cups salsa

Preheat oven to 350 degrees.

In a large bowl, combine the chicken, soup, sour cream, and onion.

In a greased 9 x 13-inch pan, layer half the chips and half the soup mixture over top. Repeat layers. Top with the cheese and bake for 30 minutes. Serve with the salsa on the side.

Southwestern Chicken Roll-Ups

Makes 4–6 *servings.*

1 cup finely crushed cheese crackers

1 envelope taco seasoning

4–6 boneless, skinless chicken breasts

4–6 slices Monterey Jack cheese

1 (4-ounce) can chopped green chiles

Preheat oven to 350 degrees.

On a plate, combine the crackers and taco seasoning. Flatten the chicken with a meat tenderizer and place 1 slice cheese and about 1 tablespoon chiles on each piece of chicken. Roll chicken and secure with a toothpick. Sprinkle chicken with the cracker mixture and place in a greased 9 x 13-inch pan. Bake uncovered for 35–40 minutes, or until chicken is done. Remove toothpicks before serving.

Family-Friendly Chicken Enchiladas

Makes 6–8 *servings.*

3 cups cooked and
   shredded chicken
2 (10.75-ounce) cans
   cream of chicken
   soup, condensed
1 cup sour cream
1 (4-ounce) can diced
   green chiles, drained
1/4 cup dried minced
   onion
2 1/2 cups grated cheddar
   cheese, divided
10 medium flour tortillas
1/3 cup milk

Preheat oven to 350 degrees.

In a bowl, combine the chicken, 1 can soup, sour cream, chiles, onion, and 1 1/2 cups cheese. Fill the tortillas with 1/3 to 1/2 cup chicken mixture. Roll filled tortillas and place seam side down in a greased 9 x 13-inch pan. Combine the remaining soup with milk and spread over rolled tortillas. Sprinkle the remaining cheese over top. Cover with aluminum foil and bake for 25 minutes. Uncover and bake for 5–10 minutes more, or until heated through.

NOTE: You can also use 1 (10-ounce) can enchilada sauce to top the enchiladas in place of the soup-and-milk mixture.

Honey Lime Chicken Enchiladas

Makes 6–8 servings.

6 tablespoons honey

5 tablespoons lime juice
   (about 1 large lime)

1 tablespoon chili
   powder

1/2 teaspoon garlic
   powder

3 boneless, skinless
   chicken breasts,
   cooked and shredded

2 cups green enchilada
   sauce, divided

8–10 flour tortillas

2 cups grated Monterey
   Jack cheese, divided

1 cup sour cream

Preheat oven to 350 degrees.

In a large bowl, combine the honey, lime juice, chili powder, and garlic powder; toss with the shredded chicken and let marinate in refrigerator for at least 30 minutes. Pour about 1/2 cup enchilada sauce in the bottom of a greased 9 x 13-inch pan. Fill each flour tortilla with about 2 tablespoons of the chicken and cheese, making sure to save about 1 cup cheese to sprinkle over the enchiladas. Mix the remaining enchilada sauce with the sour cream and any leftover marinade. Pour the sauce over the enchiladas and sprinkle with the remaining cheese. Bake for 30 minutes, or until golden and crispy on top.

Creamy Chicken Fajita Casserole

Makes 6–8 *servings.*

1 large onion, chopped
1 large green bell
  pepper, chopped
2 tablespoons vegetable
  oil
2 cups chopped cooked
  chicken
1 (10.75-ounce) can
  cream of chicken
  soup, condensed
1 (10.75-ounce) can
  cream of mushroom
  soup, condensed
1 (10-ounce) can diced
  tomato and green
  chiles
1 teaspoon chili powder
1/4 teaspoon salt
1/4 teaspoon garlic
  powder
1/4 teaspoon pepper
12 (6-inch) corn
  tortillas, torn into
  1-inch pieces
2 cups grated cheddar
  cheese, divided

Preheat oven to 350 degrees.

Sauté the onion and bell pepper in the oil in a large skillet over medium-high heat for 5 minutes, or until tender. Stir in the chicken, soups, tomatoes, chili powder, salt, garlic powder, and pepper; remove from heat. Layer one-third of the tortilla pieces in the bottom of a lightly greased 9 x 13-inch pan. Top with one-third of chicken mixture and 2/3 cup cheese. Repeat layers twice. Bake for 30–35 minutes.

NOTE: Freeze casserole up to 1 month, if desired. Thaw in refrigerator overnight, and bake as directed.

Sweet and Spicy Chicken

Makes 4 servings.

**4 boneless, skinless
   chicken breast halves**
**1¹/₂ cups uncooked long-
   grain white rice**
1¹/₂ cups salsa
**3 tablespoons packed
   light brown sugar**
**1 tablespoon Dijon-style
   mustard**

Preheat oven to 375 degrees.

Place the chicken into a greased 2-quart shallow baking dish. Pour the uncooked rice around the chicken.

In a small bowl, combine the salsa, brown sugar, and mustard. Pour the mixture over the chicken and rice. Cover with aluminum foil and bake for 30–40 minutes, or until chicken is cooked through and the rice is done.

Sweet Lemony Chicken

Makes 6 *servings.*

6 boneless, skinless
chicken breasts
2 tablespoons butter or
margarine, melted
1 cup flour
1/3 cup honey
1/4 cup lemon juice
1 tablespoon soy sauce

Preheat oven to 350 degrees.

Dip the chicken in the butter and then in the flour. Place in a greased 9 x 13-inch pan. In a small bowl, combine the honey, lemon juice, and soy sauce. Pour the sauce over the chicken. Cover with aluminum foil and bake for 40 minutes, or until the chicken is done.

Mango Chicken

Makes 4 *servings.*

1 cup uncooked white
rice
2 cups water
4 boneless, skinless
chicken breasts
1 (12-ounce) jar mango
salsa

Preheat oven to 350 degrees.

In a greased 9 x 13-inch pan, combine the rice and water. Lay the chicken over the rice and then pour mango salsa over top. Cover with aluminum foil and bake for 1 hour.

Pineapple Chicken

Makes 6–8 servings.

Preheat oven to 350 degrees.

2 cups diced cooked chicken

1 (8-ounce) can crushed pineapple, with liquid

1 cup chopped celery

1 cup cooked white rice

1 (10.75-ounce) can cream of mushroom soup, condensed

1 cup mayonnaise

1 (6-ounce) can sliced water chestnuts, drained

2 cups breadcrumbs

1 tablespoon butter or margarine, melted

In a large bowl, combine all of the ingredients except the breadcrumbs and butter. Transfer the mixture to a greased 9 x 13-inch pan. Combine the breadcrumbs and butter and sprinkle over the chicken mixture. Bake for 30–45 minutes.

Crunchy Baked Chicken

Makes 4–6 servings.

3 tablespoons butter or margarine, melted

3 cups peeled and thinly sliced potatoes

1 (16-ounce) bag frozen corn

2 teaspoons salt, divided

2 teaspoons basil, divided

1 cup graham cracker crumbs

4–6 boneless, skinless chicken breasts

1/3 cup butter or margarine, melted

Preheat oven to 375 degrees.

Pour 3 tablespoons melted butter in the bottom of a 9 x 13-inch pan. Combine the potatoes and corn in the pan, and then sprinkle with 1 teaspoon salt and 1 teaspoon basil. In a small bowl, combine the cracker crumbs and remaining salt and basil. Transfer the mixture to a plate. Dip the chicken in 1/3 cup melted butter then roll in the crumb mixture, coating completely. Place the chicken over the potatoes and corn. Cover with aluminum foil and bake for 60–75 minutes, or until chicken is done and potatoes are tender. Remove from oven, uncover, and bake 10 minutes more to brown chicken.

Roasted Chicken and Vegetables

Makes 4–6 *servings.*

6–8 red potatoes, cubed

1 pound baby carrots, cut in thirds

3–4 boneless, skinless chicken breasts

1 medium onion, thinly sliced

1 envelope onion soup mix

$1/4$ cup water

Preheat oven to 350 degrees.

Layer the potatoes and carrots in bottom of a greased 9 x 13-inch pan. Place the chicken over the vegetables and the onion over the chicken. Mix together the soup mix and water; drizzle over chicken and vegetables. Cover with aluminum foil and bake for 60–65 minutes, or until chicken is done and vegetables are tender.

After Thanksgiving Layered Casserole

Makes 4–6 *servings.*

1 (6-ounce) box seasoned
  stuffing mix
3 cups chopped cooked
  turkey
2 cups turkey gravy,
  divided
2 cups mashed potatoes,
  seasoned with garlic

Preheat oven to 350 degrees.

Prepare the stuffing according to package directions. Spoon the stuffing into a greased 2-quart baking dish. Lay the turkey over the stuffing. Pour 1 cup gravy over the turkey. Spread the mashed potatoes evenly over top. Cover with the remaining gravy. Cover with aluminum foil and bake for 35–45 minutes, or until bubbly.

NOTE: Try adding $3/4$ cup frozen peas as a layer between the stuffing and the turkey.

Turkey and Stuffing Casserole

Makes 6 servings.

2 (10.75-ounce) cans cream of celery soup, condensed

1 cup milk

1/2 teaspoon black pepper

1 (16-ounce) bag frozen mixed vegetables, thawed and drained

2 1/2 cups cubed cooked turkey

1 (6-ounce) box seasoned stuffing mix*

Preheat oven to 400 degrees.

Mix together the soup, milk, pepper, vegetables, and turkey. Spread turkey mixture into a greased 9 x 13-inch pan. Prepare the stuffing according to package directions. Spoon stuffing evenly over the turkey. Bake for 25 minutes, or until heated through.

*If you prefer a thicker layer of stuffing, use 2 boxes.

Turkey and Potato Bake

Makes 4 servings.

2 cups cubed cooked
   turkey
2 medium potatoes,
   peeled and thinly
   sliced
1 medium onion, sliced
Salt and pepper, to taste
1 (10.75-ounce) can
   cream of celery soup,
   condensed
$^1/_2$ cup milk

Preheat oven to 350 degrees.

In a greased 8 x 8-inch pan, layer the turkey, potatoes, and onion. Sprinkle with salt and pepper.

In a bowl, combine the soup and milk. Pour the mixture evenly over top. Cover with aluminum foil and bake for 1 hour.

Turkey and Green Chile Tortilla Casserole

Makes 6–8 *servings.*

3 cups chopped cooked
  turkey
1 (4-ounce) can chopped
  green chiles
³/₄ cup chicken broth
2 (10.75-ounce) cans
  cream of chicken
  soup, condensed
1 medium onion,
  chopped
8–10 medium gordita-
  style flour tortillas
2 cups grated Monterey
  Jack cheese, divided

Preheat oven to 350 degrees.

In a large bowl, combine the turkey, chiles, broth, soup, and onion. Cover the bottom of a greased 9 x 13-inch pan with half the tortillas. Spread half the turkey mixture over the tortilla layer. Sprinkle half the cheese over top. Repeat layers. Bake for 25–30 minutes, or until bubbly and heated through.

Turkey and Zucchini Rice Casserole

Makes 6–8 *servings.*

1 (10.75-ounce) can cream of onion soup, condensed
1¼ cups milk
½ envelope dry onion soup mix
1 teaspoon Italian seasoning
4 cups cooked instant rice
2 small or 1 large zucchini, ends removed*
2 cups diced cooked turkey
¾ cup grated Colby Jack or cheddar cheese

Preheat oven to 350 degrees.

In a bowl, whisk together the soup, milk, dry onion soup mix, and Italian seasoning. Gently stir rice into the mixture.

Cut the zucchini into bite-sized pieces and then fold with the turkey into the rice mixture until combined. Spoon the mixture evenly into a 9 x 13-inch pan prepared with nonstick cooking spray. Sprinkle cheese over top and bake for 30 minutes.

*Yields approximately 3½–4 cups cut bite-sized pieces zucchini.

Broccoli Turkey Wild Rice

Makes 6 servings.

Preheat oven to 350 degrees.

1 (6-ounce) package long grain and wild rice mix

2½ cups cubed cooked turkey

1 (4-ounce) can sliced mushrooms, drained

1 (10.75-ounce) can cream of mushroom soup, condensed

1 cup frozen chopped broccoli

¾ cup water

2 tablespoons soy sauce

¾ cup Italian breadcrumbs

1 tablespoon butter, melted

Prepare rice according to package directions. In a large bowl, combine cooked rice, turkey, mushrooms, soup, broccoli, water, and soy sauce. Spoon mixture into a 9 x 9-inch pan prepared with nonstick cooking spray. Cover with aluminum foil and bake for 30 minutes.

Stir together breadcrumbs and melted butter in a small bowl. Uncover casserole and sprinkle buttered breadcrumbs over the top. Bake uncovered for an additional 15–20 minutes, or until bubbly. Let casserole stand for 10 minutes before serving.

Turkey Divan

Makes 4–6 *servings.*

2 cups diced cooked
   turkey
1 (10-ounce) package
   frozen broccoli
   spears, cooked
1 (10.75-ounce) can
   cream of chicken
   soup, condensed
$1/2$ cup mayonnaise
$1/2$ teaspoon lemon juice
$1/4$ teaspoon curry
   powder
$1/2$ cup grated sharp
   cheddar cheese

Preheat oven to 350 degrees.

Layer the turkey and broccoli in a greased 9 x 13-inch pan.

In a bowl, combine the soup, mayonnaise, lemon juice, and curry powder. Pour the mixture over the turkey and sprinkle with the cheese. Cover with aluminum foil and bake for 40 minutes.

Creamy Italian Turkey Casserole

Makes 4–5 servings

1½ cups cubed cooked turkey
1 (5–6-ounce) package sliced fresh mushrooms
⅓ cup chopped red bell pepper
⅓ cup chopped onion
1 (10.75-ounce) can cream of mushroom soup, condensed
½ teaspoon minced garlic
1 teaspoon Italian seasoning
⅛ teaspoon pepper
¼ cup soft breadcrumbs
1 tablespoon butter, melted
¼ teaspoon paprika

Preheat oven 350 degrees.

In a bowl, combine the turkey, mushrooms, bell pepper, onion, soup, garlic, Italian seasoning, and pepper. Spoon the mixture into a 1½- to 2-quart baking dish prepared with nonstick cooking spray.

In a small bowl, combine the breadcrumbs and butter. Sprinkle the mixture and paprika evenly over top. Bake uncovered for 25–30 minutes, or until bubbly and golden brown.

Turkey Cordon Bleu Casserole

Makes 6 servings.

4 cups cubed cooked turkey

2 cups cubed fully cooked ham

1½ cups grated Swiss cheese, divided

⅓ cup butter

¾ cup chopped onion

⅓ cup flour

¼ teaspoon salt

¼ teaspoon ground mustard

⅛ teaspoon ground nutmeg

2¼ cups milk

¾ cup crushed buttery round crackers

Preheat oven to 350 degrees.

Layer the turkey, ham, and 1 cup cheese in a 9 x 9-inch pan prepared with nonstick cooking spray.

In a 1½- to 2-quart saucepan, melt butter. Saute the onion in butter until tender. Stir in the flour, salt, ground mustard, and nutmeg until blended. Slowly stir in the milk and then bring the sauce to a boil. Lower the heat and simmer for 2 minutes, or until the sauce starts to thicken. Stir in remaining cheese and pour the sauce evenly over meat and cheese in pan.

Sprinkle crushed crackers evenly over the casserole. Cover pan with aluminum foil and bake for 15 minutes. Remove foil and continue to bake for 10–15 minutes more or until bubbly and golden brown.

Corn-Crusted Casserole

Makes 6–8 servings.

Preheat oven to 400 degrees.

2 pounds ground turkey

3 medium onions, chopped

1½ teaspoons ground cumin

1 (4-ounce) can sliced mushrooms, drained

4 (15-ounce) cans whole kernel corn, drained

1½ teaspoons basil

1 teaspoon salt

½ teaspoon pepper

3 tablespoons butter or margarine

1 tablespoon cornstarch

2 tablespoons sugar

In a frying pan, brown the turkey and onions until meat is crumbly and no longer pink; drain if necessary. Stir in the cumin. Spoon the mixture into the bottom of a greased 9 x 13-inch pan. Sprinkle the mushrooms evenly over top.

In a blender, grind the corn for 3 minutes. Pour liquefied corn into a saucepan with the basil, salt, pepper, and butter. Heat until it starts to bubble. Slowly stir in the cornstarch to thicken. Pour the mixture evenly over the turkey and sprinkle the sugar over top. Bake for 40–50 minutes, or until golden brown.

Simple Turkey Enchiladas

Makes 6–8 servings.

1 (26-ounce) can red
    enchilada sauce,
    divided
2 cups turkey roast,*
    cooked and shredded
    ahead of time
12 (1 package) 8-inch
    flour tortillas
1 (15-ounce) can refried
    beans
1 cup cooked white rice
1 (15-ounce) can white
    corn, drained and
    rinsed
1 cup shredded cheddar
    cheese
Sour Cream, chopped
    tomatoes, shredded
    lettuce for garnishes

Preheat oven to 325 degrees.

Spray the bottom of a 9 x 13 pan with nonstick cooking spray. In a large bowl, combine half of the enchilada sauce and the turkey. Take a tortilla and layer it with a spoonful each of the beans, turkey, rice, and corn. Roll it up and place in the prepared pan. Repeat for the rest of the tortillas. Cover the enchiladas with the remaining sauce, then top with cheddar cheese. Bake for 1 hour.

Serve with sour cream, tomatoes, and shredded lettuce on top.

*This recipe is a great one to use leftover turkey roast.

Family Favorites

Homemade Macaroni and Cheese

Makes 8 servings.

1 (8-ounce) package
   elbow macaroni
   (about 2 cups
   uncooked macaroni)
2 cups milk
1/4 cup all-purpose flour
1 teaspoon onion salt
2 (10-ounce) blocks
   sharp cheddar cheese,
   grated and divided
   (about 4 1/2 cups)
1 cup soft breadcrumbs
1/4 cup butter or
   margarine, melted

Preheat oven to 350 degrees.

Cook the macaroni according to package directions; drain well and set aside. Place the milk, flour, and onion salt in a quart jar; cover tightly, and shake vigorously for 1 minute.

In a large bowl, stir together the flour mixture, 3 1/2 cups cheese, and macaroni. Pour the mixture into a lightly greased 9 x 13-inch baking dish or 2 (11-inch) oval baking dishes. Sprinkle evenly with the breadcrumbs and remaining cheese; drizzle evenly with the butter. Bake for 45 minutes, or until golden brown.

Home-Style Shells and Cheese

Makes 6 servings.

1 (16-ounce) package
   small shell pasta
1 (10.75-ounce) can
   tomato soup,
   condensed
1 1/2 cups grated cheddar
   cheese, divided

Preheat oven to 350 degrees.

Cook the shells according to package directions and drain. Stir the soup and 1 cup cheddar cheese into the shells. Spread the mixture into a greased 9 x 13-inch pan. Sprinkle the remaining cheese over top. Bake for 25–30 minutes.

Easy Mac and Cheese Bake

Makes 4–6 servings.

3 cups uncooked elbow
   macaroni
1 (16-ounce) jar Ragu
   double-cheddar sauce
1 green onion, chopped
1/4 cup seasoned
   breadcrumbs

Preheat oven to 400 degrees.

Cook the macaroni according to package directions and drain. Stir in the cheddar sauce and onion. Spread the mixture into a greased 2-quart baking dish and sprinkle the breadcrumbs over top. Cover with aluminum foil and bake for 12–15 minutes. Uncover and bake for 5 minutes more.

Cheeseburger Macaroni Casserole

Makes 6–8 *servings.*

1 pound ground beef
1 tablespoon sugar
1/2 teaspoon garlic salt
2 (8-ounce) cans tomato
   sauce
2 tablespoons water
4 ounces cream cheese,
   softened
1/2 cup milk
1 cup light sour cream
1 (8-ounce) package
   elbow macaroni,
   cooked according to
   directions
2 cups grated cheddar
   cheese

Preheat oven to 350 degrees.

In a large frying pan, brown the ground beef until no longer pink; drain if necessary. Add the sugar, garlic salt, tomato sauce, and water. Simmer for 5 minutes.

In a small bowl, combine the cream cheese, milk, and sour cream until smooth.

In a greased 9 x 13-inch pan, layer half the cooked noodles, meat mixture, half the cream mixture, and 1 cup cheese. Repeat layers. Bake for 30 minutes.

Meatball and Mac Casserole

Makes 6–8 *servings.*

1 pound frozen, fully cooked meatballs (about 26 meatballs)

2 (7.25-ounce) boxes macaroni and cheese dinner

2 (10.75-ounce) cans cream of mushroom soup, condensed

1½ cups milk

¼ teaspoon pepper

¾ cup grated Parmesan cheese

Preheat oven to 350 degrees.

Cook the frozen meatballs on a baking sheet for 20 minutes. While meatballs bake, cook the macaroni according to package directions; drain the water from the pan. Stir into the macaroni the soup, milk, pepper, and cheese packets. Place the meatballs in a 9 x 13-inch pan prepared with nonstick cooking spray. Spoon macaroni mixture evenly over the meatball layer. Sprinkle the Parmesan cheese over top. Bake uncovered for 20–25 minutes.

Stuffed Taco Pasta Shells

Makes 6–8 servings.

1 pound ground beef
1 envelope taco
   seasoning mix
1³/₄ cups salsa, divided
1 (12-ounce) package
   jumbo pasta shells,
   cooked and drained
1¹/₂ cups grated Mexican-
   blend cheese

Preheat oven to 350 degrees.

In a large frying pan, brown the ground beef until no longer pink; drain if necessary. Stir in the taco seasoning and ³/₄ cup salsa; simmer for 2 minutes. Remove from heat. Fill the cooked pasta shells with 1 tablespoon of the meat mixture. Lay the stuffed shells in the bottom of a greased 9 x 13-inch baking dish. Spoon the remaining salsa over shells and top with the cheese. Cover pan with aluminum foil. Bake for 30 minutes, or until hot and the cheese has melted.

Traditional Stuffed Pasta Shells

Makes 6 servings.

1 (16-ounce) container cottage cheese

1 egg, slightly beaten

2 cups grated mozzarella cheese

1 (12-ounce) package jumbo pasta shells, cooked and drained

1 (26-ounce) jar spaghetti sauce

Preheat oven to 350 degrees.

In a bowl, combine the cottage cheese, egg, and mozzarella. Stuff the shells with the cheese mixture, about 2–3 tablespoons per shell. Place the shells in a lightly greased 9 x 13-inch pan. Pour the spaghetti sauce over top. Cover with aluminum foil and bake for 45 minutes, or until sauce is bubbly.

Beefy Stuffed Manicotti

Makes 6–8 *servings.*

1 (26-ounce) jar spaghetti sauce, divided
1 (16-ounce) container cottage cheese
2 cups grated mozzarella cheese, divided
1/2 cup grated Parmesan cheese
1 egg, beaten
1 teaspoon dried oregano
1 pound ground beef, browned and drained
1 (8-ounce) package manicotti pasta, cooked and drained

Preheat oven to 350 degrees.

Pour about 1 cup spaghetti sauce into a greased 9 x 13-inch pan. Spread the sauce to cover the bottom of the pan. Stir the cottage cheese, 1 cup mozzarella cheese, Parmesan cheese, egg, and oregano into the warm meat. Stuff the manicotti with the meat and cheese mixture. Lay the stuffed pasta in the prepared pan. Spread the remaining spaghetti sauce over the shells. Sprinkle the remaining cheese over top. Cover with aluminum foil and bake for 40 minutes. Uncover and bake for 5–10 minutes more.

NOTE: To make this recipe even easier, use a cake decorating bag or a plastic sandwich bag with the corner cut off to pipe the manicotti filling into the pasta.

Lasagna Roll-Ups

Makes 6 servings.

¹/₂ pound ground beef
1 small onion, chopped
1 teaspoon garlic salt
1 (26-ounce) jar chunky spaghetti sauce, divided
2 cups Italian-blend grated cheese, divided
8 lasagna noodles, cooked and drained

Preheat oven to 375 degrees.

In a large frying pan, brown the ground beef and onion until meat is no longer pink; drain if necessary. Remove from heat. Sprinkle the meat with the garlic salt. Add ¹/₂ cup spaghetti sauce. Let mixture cool and then add 1 cup cheese. Spread 1 cup spaghetti sauce into bottom of a 9 x 9-inch pan.

On a clean work surface, spoon ¹/₂ cup meat mixture down the center of each lasagna noodle; roll up and place seam side down in the pan. Spread remaining sauce over roll-ups. Cover with aluminum foil and bake for 35 minutes, or until heated through. Sprinkle with remaining cheese. Bake for 5 minutes more, or until cheese melts. Let stand for 5 minutes before serving.

NOTE: You may want to cook extra lasagna noodles in case any break.

Easy Lasagna

Preheat oven to 350 degrees.

1 egg, beaten
1/4 cup grated Parmesan
    cheese
1 1/2 teaspoons Italian
    seasoning
1 (16-ounce) container
    cottage cheese,
    divided
2 cups grated mozzarella
    cheese, divided
1 pound ground beef
1 medium onion,
    chopped
1/2 cup water
2 (26-ounce) cans
    chunky spaghetti
    sauce, divided
1 (12-ounce) box
    oven-ready lasagna
    noodles, uncooked

In a bowl, combine the egg, Parmesan cheese, Italian seasoning, cottage cheese, and 1 cup mozzarella cheese; set aside.

In a large frying pan, brown the beef and onion together until done; drain if necessary. Add the water and all but 1 cup spaghetti sauce to beef. Spread the reserved sauce into the bottom of a greased 9 x 13-inch pan. Layer 5–6 lasagna noodles over sauce in pan, overlapping or breaking to fit, if necessary. Spread half the cheese mixture over the noodles. Spoon a third of the beef mixture over the cheese. Repeat layers once. Add one more layer of 5–6 noodles and spoon remaining beef mixture over top. Cover with aluminum foil and bake for 50 minutes. Sprinkle the remaining mozzarella cheese over top. Let stand for 5 minutes before serving.

Kids' Favorite Lasagna

Makes 8 servings.

1 pound ground beef,
   browned and drained
1½ teaspoons Italian
   seasoning
1 (16-ounce) container
   cottage cheese
1 egg
2 cups grated mozzarella
   cheese, divided
¾ cup water, divided
2 (26-ounce) jars
   spaghetti sauce,
   any variety, divided
1 (12-ounce) box
   oven-ready lasagna
   noodles, uncooked
1 (3.5-ounce) package
   sliced pepperoni

Preheat oven to 350 degrees.

Season the beef with the Italian seasoning; set aside.

In a bowl, combine the cottage cheese, egg, and 1 cup mozzarella cheese. Add ½ cup water and all but 1 cup spaghetti sauce to beef. Spread the reserved sauce into the bottom of a greased 9 x 13-inch pan. Layer 5–6 lasagna noodles over sauce in pan, overlapping or breaking to fit, if necessary. Spread half the cheese mixture over the noodles. Spoon a third of the beef mixture over the cheese. Top with a layer of pepperoni slices. Repeat layers once. Add one more layer of 5–6 noodles and spoon remaining beef mixture over top. Drizzle remaining water over top. Cover with aluminum foil and bake for 50 minutes. Uncover and sprinkle remaining cheese over top. Bake uncovered for 5 minutes more. Let stand 5 minutes before serving.

Ziti and Meatball Casserole

Makes 8 servings.

20 frozen, fully cooked
   meatballs
1 (16-ounce) package
   ziti or other pasta
1 (26-ounce) jar
   spaghetti sauce,
   any variety
$^1/_2$ teaspoon minced
   garlic
2 cups grated mozzarella
   cheese, divided
Chopped fresh basil or
   parsley, optional

Preheat oven to 350 degrees.

Heat the meatballs according to package directions. Cook the pasta according to package directions and drain.

In a bowl, combine the spaghetti sauce, garlic, meatballs, and half the cheese. Spoon the mixture into a 9 x 13-inch pan prepared with nonstick cooking spray. Bake for 20 minutes. Sprinkle the remaining cheese over top and bake for 5 minutes more. Garnish with the basil or parsley, if desired.

Baked Mostaccioli

Makes 6–8 servings.

Preheat oven to 350 degrees.

1 pound ground beef,
    cooked and drained
1½ (26-ounce) jars
    spaghetti sauce
1 (12-ounce) package
    mostaccioli pasta
2 cups grated
    mozzarella cheese
⅓ cup grated Parmesan
    cheese

Combine the beef and spaghetti sauce; set aside. Cook the pasta according to package directions and drain.

In a greased 9 x 13-inch pan, layer half each of the pasta, beef mixture, and mozzarella cheese. Repeat layers, and then sprinkle the Parmesan cheese over top. Cover with aluminum foil and bake for 40 minutes. Uncover and bake for 10 minutes more.

Baked Ravioli Alfredo

Makes 6 servings.

Preheat oven to 350 degrees.

1 (25-ounce) bag frozen
    Italian sausage
    ravioli
1 (16-ounce) bag frozen
    broccoli florets
1 (16-ounce) jar Alfredo
    sauce
¾ cup milk
¼ cup seasoned
    breadcrumbs

Place the frozen ravioli into the bottom of a greased 9 x 13-inch pan. Spread the broccoli over top. Pour the Alfredo sauce over the broccoli. Drizzle milk evenly over top. Cover with aluminum foil and bake for 50 minutes. Uncover and sprinkle the breadcrumbs over top. Bake uncovered for 10 minutes more, or until heated through.

Rotini Bake

12 ounces uncooked rotini pasta, cooked and drained according to directions
1 pound ground beef
1 (26-ounce) jar spaghetti sauce
2 eggs, slightly beaten
1 (16-ounce) container cottage cheese
2 cups grated mozzarella cheese, divided
1/2 cup grated Parmesan cheese

Cook pasta. Drain and set aside. In a frying pan, brown and drain beef; stir in the spaghetti sauce.

In a large bowl, combine the eggs, cottage cheese, 1 cup mozzarella cheese, and Parmesan cheese. Gently fold the cooked pasta into the cheese mixture. Spread a third of the beef mixture over the bottom of a greased 9 x 13-inch pan. Place half the pasta mixture over the beef. Layer another third of the beef mixture over the noodles. Layer the remaining noodles over top, followed by the remaining beef mixture. Cover with aluminum foil and bake for 40 minutes. Uncover and sprinkle the remaining mozzarella cheese over top. Return to oven and bake for 5–10 minutes more, or until cheese is melted.

Chilighetti

1 pound ground beef,
   browned and drained
1 (8-ounce) package
   spaghetti, cooked
   and drained
1/2 cup chopped onion
1 cup sour cream
2 (8-ounce) cans tomato
   sauce
1 (4-ounce) can sliced
   mushrooms
2 (15-ounce) cans chili,
   any type
1 clove garlic, minced
2 cups grated cheddar
   cheese

Preheat oven to 350 degrees.

In a large bowl, combine all of the ingredients except the cheese. Transfer mixture to a greased 9 x 13-inch pan. Top with the cheese. Bake for 20 minutes.

Sausage Spaghetti Casserole

Makes 6–8 *servings.*

1 pound sausage

1 medium onion, chopped

1 (26-ounce) jar spaghetti sauce

½ cup water

1 (16-ounce) package spaghetti noodles, cooked and drained

¼ cup butter or margarine, melted

3 eggs, beaten

½ cup grated Parmesan cheese

2 cups grated mozzarella cheese, divided

1 (16-ounce) container cottage cheese

Preheat oven to 350 degrees.

In a frying pan, brown the sausage and onion; drain if necessary. Stir the spaghetti sauce and water into the sausage mixture. Let sauce simmer over low heat for 5 minutes.

In a bowl, combine the spaghetti, butter, eggs, Parmesan, and half the mozzarella cheese. Spread the noodle mixture into a greased 9 x 13-inch pan. Evenly spread the cottage cheese over the noodles. Spread the spaghetti sauce mixture evenly over top. Sprinkle remaining cheese over sauce. Cover with aluminum foil and bake for 25 minutes. Uncover and bake for 10–15 minutes more.

Italian Macaroni Bake

Makes 6 *servings.*

8 ounces uncooked
   elbow macaroni
1 pound ground beef,
   browned and drained
Salt and pepper, to taste
1 (14-ounce) jar pizza
   sauce, divided
1 (4-ounce) can sliced
   mushrooms, divided
2 cups grated mozzarella
   cheese, divided

Preheat oven to 350 degrees.

Cook macaroni according to package directions and drain.

Season the cooked beef with the salt and pepper. Place half the macaroni into the bottom of a greased 2-quart baking dish. Layer half each of the beef, pizza sauce, mushrooms, and cheese. Place remaining macaroni over top and repeat layers. Cover with aluminum foil and bake for 20 minutes. Uncover and bake for 5–10 minutes more, or until cheese is melted.

Buried Pepperoni Supreme Pizza

Makes 6–8 *servings.*

2 (13.8-ounce) tubes refrigerated pizza crust dough
2 (8-ounce) cans tomato sauce, divided
1 teaspoon Italian seasoning
24 slices pepperoni
1 (4-ounce) can mushroom pieces, drained
1 (3.8-ounce) can sliced olives, drained
2 cups grated mozzarella cheese, divided

Preheat oven to 375 degrees.

Spread 1 pizza crust over the bottom and up the sides of a lightly greased 9 x 13-inch pan. Spread 1$\frac{1}{2}$ cans tomato sauce over top. Sprinkle the Italian seasoning over the sauce, and then layer the pepperoni, mushrooms, and olives over the sauce. Sprinkle 1$\frac{1}{2}$ cups cheese over top. Place the remaining pizza crust over top. Pinch the lower and upper dough crust together. Cut four 1-inch slits in top of crust. Spread the remaining sauce and cheese over top. Bake for 30 minutes, or until crust is golden brown and done in the center.

Deep Dish Pizza

Makes 6–8 *servings.*

1 (13.8-ounce) tube
   refrigerated pizza
   crust dough
1 (8-ounce) can tomato
   sauce
1 1/2 teaspoons Italian
   seasoning
1 pound sausage,
   browned and drained
1 (3.8-ounce) can sliced
   olives, drained
1/2 onion, thinly sliced
1/3 cup chopped green
   bell pepper
1 1/2 cups grated
   mozzarella cheese

Preheat oven to 425 degrees.

Press the pizza crust over the bottom and halfway up the sides of a lightly greased 9 x 13-inch pan. Bake for 9 minutes. Spread the sauce over the crust. Sprinkle the Italian seasoning and sausage over sauce, followed by the olives, onion, and bell pepper. Sprinkle the cheese over top. Bake for 7–11 minutes, or until cheese is melted and crust is golden brown.

Canadian Bacon Pizza Bake

Makes 6 *servings.*

2 (7.5-ounce) tubes
    refrigerated
    buttermilk biscuits
1 (14-ounce) jar pizza
    sauce
1 cup grated Italian-
    blend cheese
15–20 slices Canadian
    bacon
1½ cups grated
    mozzarella cheese

Preheat oven to 375 degrees.

Separate the biscuits and then cut each one into 4 pieces. Place in a large bowl and toss with the pizza sauce and Italian-blend cheese. Place the mixture into a greased 9 x 13-inch pan. Place the Canadian bacon slices evenly over the mixture. Sprinkle the mozzarella cheese over top. Bake for 20–25 minutes, or until biscuits are done.

Layered Mexican Pizza

Makes 6 servings.

1 (8-ounce) tube refrigerated crescent roll dough
1½ pounds ground beef
1 medium onion, chopped
1 envelope taco seasoning
1 cup salsa
1½ cups grated Mexican-blend cheese
1 (10-ounce) bag shredded lettuce
2 Roma tomatoes, diced
2 cups crushed nacho cheese tortilla chips

Preheat oven to 350 degrees.

Roll out crescent dough and press seams together. Cover the bottom of a greased 9 x 13-inch pan with the dough. Bake for 10–14 minutes, or until light golden brown.

In a frying pan, brown the beef and onion together until done; drain if necessary. Stir the taco seasoning and salsa into beef. Spread the mixture over the baked crust. Sprinkle the cheese over top. Bake for 2–5 minutes, or until cheese is melted. Layer the lettuce, tomatoes, and crushed chips over top. Serve immediately.

Mashed Potato Pizza

Makes 6–8 servings.

1 (10-ounce) tube pizza crust dough

2 cups grated cheddar cheese, divided

1 (3-ounce) jar real bacon bits, divided

4 servings instant mashed potato flakes, prepared according to directions

¼ cup chopped green onions

Sour cream

Preheat oven to 400 degrees.

Press the pizza crust into a lightly greased 9 x 13-inch pan. Bake for 8 minutes; set aside.

Stir half the cheese and half the bacon bits into the warm potatoes. Spread the mixture over the partially baked crust. Sprinkle the green onions, remaining bacon bits, and remaining cheese over the potato layer. Bake for 10–12 minutes more, or until cheese is completely melted. Garnish with sour cream.

NOTE: If using a pizza crust that covers a baking sheet, prepare 6 servings of instant mashed potatoes instead of 4.

Potato Crust Pizza

Makes 6–8 *servings.*

12–16 ounces ground
 sausage
1 small onion, chopped
2½–3 cups russet
 potatoes, peeled and
 thinly sliced
1 (26-ounce) jar chunky
 vegetable spaghetti
 sauce
2 cups grated mozzarella
 cheese
Grated Parmesan cheese

Preheat oven to 350 degrees.

Brown together the sausage and onion. Spread the potato slices in the bottom of a greased 9 x 13-inch pan. Spread the sausage and onion over top. Cover evenly with the spaghetti sauce. Cover with aluminum foil and bake for 30–35 minutes. Remove from oven and sprinkle the mozzarella cheese over top. Bake for 10–15 minutes more, or until cheese is melted and sauce is bubbly. Garnish with the Parmesan cheese.

NOTE: Add pepperoni, olive, or mushroom slices before spaghetti sauce. Ground beef or turkey can also be substituted for the sausage.

Chicago-Style Pizza Casserole

Makes 6–8 *servings.*

2 (13.8-ounce) tubes refrigerated pizza crust dough

2 cups traditional spaghetti sauce, divided

1 pound sausage, browned and drained

1/2 medium onion, chopped

2 cups grated mozzarella cheese, divided

Preheat oven to 375 degrees.

Spread 1 pizza crust over the bottom and up the sides of a lightly greased 9 x 13-inch pan. Spread 1½ cups sauce over the crust. Spread the sausage and onion over sauce. Sprinkle 1½ cups cheese over top. Place the remaining pizza crust over top and pinch dough from the lower and upper crusts together. Cut 1-inch slits in top crust. Carefully spread remaining sauce and cheese over top. Bake for 30 minutes, or until crust is golden brown and done in the center.

Pizza Puffs

Makes 6–8 servings.

Preheat oven to 400 degrees.

1 pound ground beef,
   browned and drained
1 (15-ounce) can pizza
   sauce
2 (7.5-ounce) tubes
   refrigerated biscuits
2 cups grated mozzarella
   cheese
1/2 cup grated cheddar
   cheese

In a bowl, combine the beef and pizza sauce. Cut the biscuits into 4 pieces each and place in a greased 9 x 13-inch pan. Pour beef mixture over top. Bake uncovered for 20–25 minutes. Sprinkle the cheese over top. Bake for 3–7 minutes more, or until cheese is melted.

Fiesta Chicken Casserole

Makes 4–6 servings.

Preheat oven to 350 degrees.

2 cups uncooked small
   shell pasta
2 cups chopped cooked
   chicken
1 (16-ounce) jar medium
   salsa
2 cups grated Mexican-
   blend cheese

Cook the pasta according to package directions and drain. Combine all of the ingredients in a greased 9 x 13-inch pan. Cover with aluminum foil and bake for 20–25 minutes, or until heated through.

Corn Bread Chicken Casserole

Makes 6 servings.

4 cups uncooked egg noodles

3 cups chopped cooked chicken

2 (10.75-ounce) cans cream of celery soup, condensed

1 (15-ounce) can cream-style corn

2 cups grated cheddar cheese

1 (8.5-ounce) package corn bread mix

Preheat oven to 350 degrees.

Boil the noodles for 5–7 minutes, or until done; drain. Mix the noodles with the chicken, soup, corn, and cheese. Pour noodle mixture into a greased 9 x 13-inch pan.

In a bowl, combine corn bread mix and ingredients listed on the package according to package directions. Spoon the batter over the noodle mixture. Bake for 25–30 minutes, or until corn bread is golden brown.

Chicken Tetrazzini

Makes 6–8 servings.

Preheat oven to 350 degrees.

1 (7-ounce) package uncooked dried spaghetti, broken in half

5 tablespoons butter, divided

2 cups sliced fresh mushrooms

1/4 cup chopped green bell pepper

1/4 cup chopped onion

1/4 cup all-purpose flour

2 cups milk

2 cups diced cooked chicken

2 teaspoons instant chicken bouillon granules

1/4 teaspoon pepper

1/2 cup grated cheddar cheese

1/2 cup grated Parmesan cheese

Cook the spaghetti according to package directions; drain and keep warm. Melt 1 tablespoon butter in a 12-inch skillet until sizzling; add the mushrooms, bell pepper, and onion. Cook over medium heat, stirring occasionally until crisp-tender, about 4–5 minutes; set aside. Melt the remaining butter in a 3-quart saucepan; stir in the flour and cook for 1 minute. Stir in the milk with a whisk until smooth. Continue cooking, stirring constantly, until mixture comes to a boil, about 6–8 minutes. Remove from heat. Stir in the cooked spaghetti and vegetables, chicken, bouillon granules, and pepper. Spoon into a greased 2-quart casserole or 9 x 13-inch baking dish. Sprinkle with the cheeses. Bake for 25–30 minutes, or until heated through.

Ham and Cheddar Noodle Casserole

Makes 4–6 *servings.*

1 (12-ounce) bag egg
    noodles
¼ cup diced green bell
    pepper
½ medium onion
1 tablespoon olive oil
1 (10.5-ounce) can
    cream of golden
    mushroom soup,
    condensed
⅔ cup milk
1½ cups diced fully
    cooked ham
2 cups grated cheddar
    cheese

Preheat oven to 400 degrees.

Cook the noodles according to package directions and drain.

In a frying pan, saute the bell pepper and onion in the oil until onion is translucent. Stir into the noodles the soup, milk, ham, vegetables, and cheese. Spread the noodle mixture into a greased 2-quart baking dish. Bake for 15 minutes, or until heated through.

Paula's Turketti

Makes 6–8 servings.

1 (10.75-ounce) can
   cream of mushroom
   soup, condensed
1/2 cup water
2 cups cubed cooked
   turkey
1 1/2 cups spaghetti,
   broken, cooked, and
   drained
1/3 cup chopped green
   bell pepper
1/2 cup chopped onion
1/2 teaspoon salt
1/4 teaspoon black
   pepper
2 cups grated cheddar
   cheese, divided

Preheat oven to 350 degrees.

In a large bowl, combine the soup and water. Stir in all of the remaining ingredients except 1 cup cheese. Spread mixture in a greased 9 x 13-inch pan. Sprinkle the remaining cheese over top. Bake for 45 minutes.

Poppy Seed Casserole

Makes 6–8 servings.

1½ pounds ground turkey
1 green or red bell pepper, chopped
3 (8-ounce) cans tomato sauce
½ teaspoon salt
½ teaspoon black pepper
1 (8-ounce) package cream cheese, cubed
½ cup sour cream
1 cup cottage cheese
1 tablespoon poppy seeds
1 (12–18-ounce) bag rotini pasta, cooked and drained
1 teaspoon Italian seasoning
½ cup grated Parmesan cheese

Preheat oven to 350 degrees.

Brown the turkey and bell pepper together until turkey is done; drain off liquid. Add the tomato sauce, salt, and pepper and simmer over low heat.

In a bowl, combine the cream cheese, sour cream, cottage cheese, and poppy seeds; mix with the hot noodles. Place the noodle mixture into the bottom of a greased 9 x 13-inch pan and top with turkey mixture. Cover with aluminum foil and bake for 30 minutes. Uncover and sprinkle with the Italian seasoning and Parmesan cheese; bake for 5–10 minutes more.

Turkey Noodle Casserole

Makes 4–6 *servings.*

1 (12-ounce) bag egg noodles

1 (10.75-ounce) can cream of celery soup, condensed

½ cup milk

1 (5-ounce) can turkey, drained

2 cups grated cheddar cheese

½ cup crushed potato chips

Preheat oven to 400 degrees.

Cook the noodles according to package directions and drain. Stir the soup, milk, turkey, and cheese into hot noodles. Spread the noodle mixture into a greased 2-quart baking dish. Bake for 15 minutes. Top with crushed potato chips and bake for 3–5 minutes more.

Baked Pasta with Smoked Sausage

Makes 10–12 *servings.*

1 tablespoon olive oil
1 medium red onion, chopped
4 cloves garlic, minced
1 (14.5-ounce) can diced tomatoes
1 (14.5-ounce) can crushed tomatoes
1/2 teaspoon dried oregano
1/2 teaspoon dried basil
1/2 cup heavy cream
Salt and pepper, to taste
1 (16-ounce) package rigatoni
1 (12-ounce) package precooked smoked sausage, halved lengthwise and sliced into 1/4-inch pieces
1 (10-ounce) bag frozen baby spinach, thawed and drained well
1 (8-ounce) block mozzarella cheese, half cut into 1/2-inch cubes and half grated
1/4 cup grated Parmesan cheese

Preheat oven to 400 degrees.

Bring a large pot of salted water to a boil.

Heat the oil in a large skillet over medium heat. Add the onion; cook until clear, about 3 minutes. Stir in the garlic and cook for another minute. Stir in the tomatoes, oregano, and basil; simmer for 8–10 minutes. Add the cream; cook until warmed through, about 5 minutes. Season sauce with salt and pepper to taste.

Cook the pasta in the boiling water according to package instructions. Drain and return pasta to pot. Add the tomato sauce, sausage, spinach, and cubed mozzarella to the pot; toss to coat. Season with salt and pepper. Scoop the mixture into a greased 9 x 13-inch pan. Top with the grated mozzarella and Parmesan cheeses. Bake until browned and edges are crisp, about 20–30 minutes.

Traditional Tuna Noodle Casserole

Makes 4–6 *servings.*

1 (12-ounce) bag egg
   noodles
1 (10.75-ounce) can
   cream of mushroom
   soup, condensed
½ cup milk
1 (6-ounce) can tuna,
   drained
2 cups grated cheddar
   cheese
½ cup crushed cheddar
   and sour cream
   potato chips

Preheat oven to 400 degrees.

Cook the noodles according to package directions and drain. Stir the soup, milk. tuna, and cheese into noodles. Spread the mixture into a greased 2-quart baking dish. Bake for 15 minutes. Top with the crushed chips and bake for 3–5 minutes more.

NOTE: One cup cooked peas can be added to the noodle mixture before baking.

Crescent Tuna Casserole

Makes 5–6 *servings.*

1 (16-ounce) jar Alfredo
  sauce
1 (9-ounce) bag frozen
  peas, thawed
1 (4-ounce) can sliced
  mushrooms, drained
2 (5-ounce) cans tuna,
  drained
1 (2-ounce) jar chopped
  pimientos, drained
1 (8-ounce) tube
  refrigerated crescent
  roll dough

Preheat oven to 375 degrees.

In a 3-quart saucepan, combine the Alfredo sauce, peas, and mushrooms. Cook over medium heat until bubbly. Fold in the tuna and pimientos. Immediately pour the mixture into an 8 x 11-inch casserole dish. Unroll the crescent dough. Press the edges and perforations together to form 1 large rectangle. Place the dough rectangle over the sauce mixture. Bake for 14–18 minutes, or until top is golden brown.

Crabmeat Shells and Cheese

Makes 6–8 *servings.*

1/2 cup diced green bell pepper

2 tablespoons thinly sliced green onion

2 tablespoons butter

2 tablespoons flour

1/2 teaspoon salt

2 cups milk

3/4 cup salsa

1 teaspoon dried parsley

1 3/4 cups shredded Pepper Jack or Monterey Jack cheese, divided

3 1/2 cups medium shell pasta, cooked and drained

1 pound imitation crabmeat, flaked

Preheat oven to 350 degrees.

In a 3-quart saucepan, saute the bell pepper and onion in butter until tender. Add the flour and salt, stirring until blended. Slowly stir in the milk. Bring to a boil and stir bubbly sauce for 2 minutes until it thickens. Stir in the salsa and parsley. Remove pan from heat and immediately stir in 1 cup cheese. Fold in the cooked shells and crabmeat. Spoon the mixture into a 9 x 13-inch baking pan prepared with nonstick cooking spray. Cover with aluminum foil and bake for 20 minutes. Remove cover, sprinkle remaining cheese over top, and bake uncovered for 5–10 minutes more.

Fish and Cheesy Pasta Casserole

Makes 5 servings.

16 ounces curly pasta, cooked and drained

1 (16-ounce) jar Ragu double-cheddar sauce

5 frozen battered fish fillets

Preheat oven to 375 degrees.

Cook the pasta according to package directions and drain. Place the pasta in a greased 9 x 13-inch pan. Stir in the cheddar sauce. Place the fish over top. Bake uncovered for 30 minutes.

Tuna and Tater Tot Casserole

Makes 6 servings.

1 (32-ounce) bag frozen tater tots

1 (6-ounce) can tuna, drained

1 (10.75-ounce) can cream of chicken soup, condensed

1/2 cup milk

1 1/2 cups grated cheddar cheese

Preheat oven to 350 degrees.

Place the tater tots in a greased 2-quart baking dish. Combine the tuna, soup, and milk. Pour over the tater tots and then sprinkle with the cheese. Cover and bake for 1 hour.

NOTE: Canned chicken or ham may be substituted for the tuna.

Garlic Parmesan Salmon with Wild Rice

1 (6-ounce) box long-
    grain and wild rice
    mix
2 tablespoons
    mayonnaise
1 clove garlic, minced
2 tablespoons grated
    Parmesan cheese
1/4 teaspoon crushed red
    pepper flakes
2 fresh salmon fillets
3/4 cup crushed butter
    crackers

Preheat oven to 400 degrees.

Cook the wild rice according to package directions. While the rice is cooking, mix together the mayonnaise, garlic, Parmesan cheese, and pepper flakes. Spray a 9 x 13-inch baking pan with non-stick spray; place the salmon in the pan. Spread the garlic-cheese mixture over the salmon. Sprinkle the cracker crumbs over the fillets. Bake uncovered for 15 minutes, or until the cracker crumbs are browned. Remove the fillets from the baking pan and lay over the wild rice. Serve immediately. Makes 4–6 servings.

Index